ADVANCE PRAISE FOR
VETERANS' LAMENT

"*Veterans' Lament*, written by two fellow Marine veterans Oliver North and David Goetsch, does Americans a great service by exposing the left's strategy of denying and revising our historical record to provide a false foundation for their 'progressive' narrative. Evidence of the Christian foundation of our country is overwhelming and undeniable, but the left's intentional removal of that evidence has set America up for a militantly secular, anti-Christian, unlimited government. This book can help us avoid that tragedy and rebuild our sabotaged foundation."
—ARCHIE P. JONES, Ph.D., co-author of *Liberal Tyranny in Higher Education* and U.S. Marine Corps veteran

"In light of the polarization we see all around us, I recommend *Veterans' Lament*, especially to young people at any point on the political spectrum. Here is an accessible volume in which you hear directly from many veterans who have earned the right to be heard. You will find the words, heartfelt concerns, and commitment of those who have gone before and sacrificed a great deal to secure the blessing of liberty we enjoy and have inherited as a fragile stewardship."
—BEN ROSSELL, Pastor, Trinity Presbyterian Church/Communion of Reformed Evangelical Churches

"*Veterans' Lament* is an excellent new book by two Marine veterans, Lt. Col. Oliver North and Dr. David Goetsch. It makes the important point that appeasement and compromise have weakened the soul of our nation. The rights of our military personnel, students, and citizens in general are being methodically stripped away by a vocal minority."
—Lt. Col. (Retired) SEAN ALAND, U.S. Air Force

"*Veterans' Lament* is a must-read, not just for military veterans and their families, but for all Americans who are concerned about our nation's future. Veterans are rightly concerned about the internal attacks on our culture, values, and liberty by anti-Christian progressives who distort our history. Lt. Col. Oliver North and Dr. David Goetsch deliver a book that will equip you to help restore our culture and the liberty for which our veterans fought."
— JENNIE JONES, Professor of Political Science and
    American history

"This excellent new book by Oliver North and David Goetsch is a thought-provoking read for all Americans of all political affiliations and persuasions."
— DAVID KING, Senior Non-Commissioned Officer (Retired),
    U.S. Air Force

"In this new book, Oliver North and Dr. Goetsch demonstrate in clear terms why I have great concerns for future generations unless our country is turned around and our national sovereignty respected once again."
— DR. CHARLES E. "Chuck" MERKEL, Jr., Major (Retired),
    U.S. Army

Also by Oliver L. North

Under Fire: An American Story
The Rifleman

Also by David Goetsch

Christian Women on the Job:
Excelling at Work without Compromising Your Faith

VETERANS' LAMENT

IS THIS THE AMERICA
OUR HEROES FOUGHT FOR?

★ ★ ★

OLIVER L. NORTH
AND
DAVID GOETSCH

FIDELIS
BOOKS

A FIDELIS BOOKS BOOK
An Imprint of Post Hill Press

ISBN: 978-1-64293-501-1
ISBN (eBook): 978-1-64293-502-8

Veterans' Lament:
Is This the America Our Heroes Fought For?
© 2020 by Oliver L. North and David Goetsch
All Rights Reserved

Cover Design by David Ter-Avanesyan
Cover Photo by Harry Benson

Unless otherwise noted, all biblical quotations are from the English
Standard Version. Scripture quoted from the English Standard
Version is copyright © 2004 Crossway Bibles, a publishing ministry
of Good News Publishers. Used by permission. All rights reserved.

Post Hill Press
New York • Nashville
posthillpress.com

Published in the United States of America

★ ★ ★

*To our military heroes past and present for answering
our nation's call and serving with honor*

For Betsy
A woman who fears the Lord is to be praised…

"Many women do noble things, but you surpass them all."
PROVERBS 31:29

★ ★ ★

★ ★ ★

From David Goetsch:

*To my beautiful wife, Deby.
With all of my love.
God bless you for loving me all these years.*

★ ★ ★

TABLE OF CONTENTS

Is This the America We Fought For?

The premise: "*Is one country more exceptional than others? Is any country or government worth risking one's life, limbs, and treasure? As a descendant of those who have served since the French and Indian War and as a combat-wounded veteran, I suppose most modern-day veterans and many civilians ask these questions. But one wonders if previous generations questioned the cost of freedom. The survival and nature of our republic depend on the answers to these questions supported by a broad consensus of all Americans.*"

—*PATT MANEY, U.S. Army, 1970–2007*

*T*he veteran who expresses the premise for this chapter is Judge (retired) Patt Maney. Judge Maney is also a retired Army Brigadier General, a veteran wounded by an improvised explosive device (IED), a Purple Heart recipient, and a member of the Florida Veterans' Hall of Fame who retired from the U.S. Army in 2007. General Maney's active and reserve duty totals almost thirty-seven years. After initial active duty, Maney attended law school and served in the Ready Reserve. After graduating from law school, he remained in the Reserve. Judge Maney practiced law for fifteen years before being appointed to the bench as Okaloosa County Court judge in 1989. He retired from the bench in 2018 after almost twenty-nine years.

As a reservist, Judge Maney had four contingency deployments, to Panama (Operation Just Cause), Haiti (Operation Uphold Democracy), Bosnia (Operation Joint Endeavor), and Afghanistan (Operation Enduring Freedom). After each deployment, he returned to the bench. The most dramatic of his deployments were in Bosnia for ten months and Afghanistan for almost seventeen months. A self-described "broken but undefeated soldier," he is a service-connected disabled veteran who was wounded by an IED in Afghanistan and spent nearly twenty months recovering at Walter Reed medical center.

In 2010, Maney was named the National Patriot of the Year by the Military Order of the Purple Heart. In 2019, he received the Medal of Honor from the National Society of the Daughters of the American Revolution. Also in 2019, he was named the National Disabled Veteran of the Year by the organization Disabled American Veterans. The Military Order of the World Wars awarded Maney the Silver Patrick Henry Award. The Florida state legislature named the Florida Veterans Treatment Court Act after him.

What is Happening to Our Country?

Judge Maney's comment about how the future of America depends on our citizens regaining a broad consensus on American exceptionalism is not just accurate, it's prescient. This issue was the subject of discussion as a large group of veterans gathered at the state Capitol waiting for the governor to induct the latest class into the Florida Veterans' Hall of Fame. Two veterans of the Korean War were talking. One of them commented wistfully that he didn't know what was happening to our country. The America he saw around him every day wasn't the country he fought for. This was a powerful statement coming from someone who, as a young man, volunteered for service in the U.S. Army and went in harm's way to defend his country. As things turned out, his statement became the genesis of this book.

These kinds of comments from military veterans are not new to us. A lot of Americans, particularly veterans, are concerned about what they view as the declining state of the nation. Progressives on the left are using all the tools available to them—the mainstream media, the entertainment industry, public education, and academia—to undermine America's Christian heritage and thereby our core values. As a result, traditional moral restraints on behavior have been pushed aside and personal responsibility is no longer considered a virtue.

As Marine Corps veterans, we have talked with thousands of other veterans over the years who are concerned about where they see our nation headed. Their concerns mirror those of the veterans we surveyed and interviewed for this book. To us, their concerns carry extra weight because they have sacrificed so much for the country they love and are concerned about. In recent years, many veterans have shared with us their concerns about the state of our nation. Many veterans wonder if the America they know and love still exists.

One veteran we interviewed said he thought America was racing down a one-way street to disaster. As we interact with veterans, they often express concerns about trends they fear are eroding the moral fabric and core values of our country, the very things that in their opinion make America a nation worth fighting for.

Veterans we talk with are concerned that politicians, the media, the entertainment industry, public education, and universities are focusing on and obsessing over the things that divide Americans rather than the things that have historically brought us together. In a nation as diverse as the United States, this is a dangerous trend. As they observe what is happening around them, many former warriors are asking the same question: Is this the America we fought for?

Veterans and other Americans who are worried about the state of the nation are right to be concerned. There is a growing divide in our country between those who still believe in the America envisioned by our founders and those who reject that vision. For example, a recent Gallup poll revealed that 76 percent of Republicans are "extremely proud" to be Americans, but only 22 percent of Democrats make this claim. This is a decline from earlier polls in which more than 50 percent of Democrats indicated they were proud to be Americans. Has America changed or have Democrats changed? Or could it be Democrats have changed America?

Increasingly, it appears progressives actually hate the America our veterans fought for and love. Listen to extreme leftists in the Democratic Party and you will have no doubt they view America's founders not as heroes or visionaries, but as male chauvinists unworthy of esteem—old white men who built a nation to benefit themselves to the exclusion of women and people of other races. In the eyes of the Democratic Party of the twenty-first century, the worst things a person can be guilty of are being conservative, Christian, male, and/or white.

As the sociopolitical gulf and tributaries dividing our country continue to grow and spread, veterans and other citizens who are proud to be Americans are facing a battle. But the battle in this case is not on foreign shores, and it doesn't involve guns, tanks, jets, or missiles. It is a battle of ideas occurring right here and right now in the United States of America. It is a battle for the soul of our nation, a battle centered on the moral foundation and core values that made our nation great. As such, it may be the most important battle Americans have ever fought since the American Revolution. It is also a battle that must be won, or people on the right, the left, and in the middle of the political spectrum, as well as people of all religions and no religion, will suffer.

Before proceeding, let us be clear about what we mean by America's moral foundation and core values, two concepts at the heart of this book. When it comes to the moral foundation of our nation, America was built not just on Plymouth Rock but on the even more solid rock of God's Word. America's heritage is a Christian heritage. Some of the earliest European settlers came to America seeking religious freedom. They wanted to be able to practice their religion without coercion or interference from whoever occupied the thrones of Europe at any given point in time. These early settlers were eventually instrumental in building a new country on this continent on a solid foundation of Christian principles. In the America envisioned by our founders, religion would not be required of citizens, but it would be encouraged, supported, and respected.

A Veteran Speaks Out

"The incivility and lack of manners I see every day trouble me. My grandfather had to tell me only once to say 'yes, sir.' We were raised to show respect for adults and people in authority. You seldom see that anymore. Shame on parents for not teaching their children manners. Shame on the rest of us for not speaking up when young people are rude or disrespectful. If we don't teach them about personal responsibility, good manners, right and wrong, and other important values, who will?"

—GREG WALDRON, U.S. Army, 1984–1988

Waldron left the Army as a non-commissioned officer (NCO) and has had a long career supporting the Air Force in test-range operations as a defense contractor.

When it comes to understanding America's core values, start with the first eight amendments in the Bill of Rights. Our core values begin with a commitment to personal liberty and individual rights. Joined with this commitment to personal liberty and individual rights are additional values such as honesty, integrity, personal responsibility, self-reliance, charity, practicality, self-improvement, equality, justice, opportunity, fair competition, a positive work ethic, the rule of law, and self-government. When you consider our nation's moral foundation and core values, it is easy to understand why the United States became the most powerful and productive nation in the history of the world. Unfortunately, the very things that made America great are now under attack by people who benefit immensely from them.

Ironically, while the American military fights to defend the freedoms spelled out in the Bill of Rights, progressives on the left are taking advantage of those rights to attack what our soldiers, sailors, airmen, guardsmen, and Marines are fighting for. Hence, the term they have chosen for themselves—"progressives"—is itself a misnomer. Is there anything progressive about driving America over a moral cliff and undermining the values that make our country a nation worth fighting for? The veterans we talk with don't think so.

We live in a fallen world. Consequently, there will always be battles around the globe involving armed conflict. Further, there will always be times when the American military will have to join in those conflicts. But the battle at the heart of this book is a battle for the future of America, a battle between two competing philosophies. On one side are Americans who love our country, believe in the vision of our founders, and subscribe to the core values that made America great.

These Americans readily acknowledge our country isn't perfect and we have made mistakes, but they also acknowledge that no country works harder to correct its mistakes and strengthen its weaknesses. On the other side are progressives who believe America is an unworthy, racist, misogynist nation run by evil bigots who care nothing about everyday citizens. These so-called progressives want to recast America as a socialist utopia in which the government controls every aspect of daily life and they control the government.

Those trying to undermine our nation's moral foundation and core values mislead, misrepresent, and manipulate. Worse yet, they take advantage of the most vulnerable of our citizens, those at the bottom of the socioeconomic ladder, to advance their nefarious agenda. Rather than preserve and continually enhance a system that provides the means for people in poverty to improve their circumstances—something millions of Americans have done over the years—progressives advance an agenda that has kept people in economic bondage while creating even more poverty. The only benefit that could possibly come out of the progressive agenda is that it would solve America's border crisis. With progressives controlling our country, illegal immigrants would have to look elsewhere to escape the soul-crushing poverty and tyranny of their home nations. Why leave one socialist cesspool just to jump into another?

The progressive agenda concerns a lot of veterans who fought to preserve the things that made America what President Ronald Reagan often called a "bright shining city on a hill." One veteran we interviewed commented that if things keep going the way they are, America will no longer resemble the vision set forth by the founders, a vision so aptly captured by President Reagan's eloquent verbal imagery. This veteran said if progressives would simply observe the conditions in socialist nations, they wouldn't find anything bright or shining about them.

Because we often hear military veterans express concerns about the erosion of traditional American values, the values they defended while serving in uniform, we decided to augment the thousands of informal conversations we have had with veterans over the years with a survey and structured interviews. What follows is a list of concerns expressed to us by veterans who participated in our survey and interviews, as well as during our informal conversations over the years.

- Increasing acceptance of socialism, particularly among younger Americans

- Attacks on the Second Amendment

- Revising and falsifying America's history

- Turning away from our moral roots to secular humanism, moral relativism, and political correctness

- Politics of destruction

- Porous borders and sanctuary cities

- Coarsening of the culture (incivility, school shootings, workplace violence, and road rage)

- Anti-Christian and anti-conservative bias in schools, colleges, and the media

- Disrespect for America's flag and the National Anthem

Is America Exceptional or Exceptionally Bad?

A battle is raging within our country's borders between two competing and incompatible visions of America. On one side of the sociopolitical gulf are patriots who still believe in the country envisioned by our founders, an America that stands out as exceptional in the community of nations. On the other side are those marching under many banners who believe America is exceptional only in the sense that it is exceptionally bad. These people view the United States through a lens that lets them see nothing but its warts and blemishes. To them, nothing about America is admirable or worthy of respect. Rather, America is a nation that must be torn down and rebuilt from the bottom up according to the strictures of socialism and secularism.

Whereas those who love America view such luminaries as George Washington and Thomas Jefferson as great but flawed men, progressives view them only as flawed men. To America's indigenous detractors, George Washington's contributions as commander in chief of the Army during America's War of Independence and as our first president are canceled out by the fact he owned slaves. Likewise, Thomas Jefferson's eloquent, inspiring prose in the Declaration of Independence and his service as America's third president mean nothing because he too was a slaveholder.

Hypocritically, progressives refuse to acknowledge that to this day, they and all Americans benefit immensely from the sacrifices these two founders and their compatriots made in establishing our country. It also begs the question, if these America haters feel themselves qualified to make such judgments because they are perfect in every way—these people who hold a sign protesting "inequality" in one hand and one to protect abortion in the other.

Americans who still believe in the country envisioned by the founders are able to acknowledge both the contributions and shortcomings of Washington, Jefferson, and other giants from our past. Traditionalists are proud of the progress America has made in overcoming past inequalities. What is ironic about the negative, pessimistic, destructive view of progressives is that their policies and practices are what lead to and perpetuate some of America's worst warts and blemishes. It's as if they expect Americans to apologize for the problems they have and are causing themselves. This is why it is important to understand the exceptional nature of America.

America is not exceptional simply because it has such a high standard of living, although this is one of the main reasons immigrants have long sought American citizenship. Our country is not exceptional simply because it has the strongest military in the world, although millions of people around the globe owe their freedom to this fact. America is exceptional less for what it is at any given point in time than for what it has strived to be since its inception. America is not just a geographic location on a map; it's an idea—an idea that grew out of Christian principles and corresponding values. America aspires to be a bastion of individual freedom, self-government, unlimited opportunity, religious liberty, unparalleled equality, and economic prosperity. This aspiration and the fact we are committed to achieving it are what make America exceptional.

Unfortunately, these elements of our national aspiration are under attack by progressives, whose agenda is anything but progressive. This is what concerns the veterans we talk with. They fear the day may come when our country is ruled by people who do not believe in American exceptionalism. One veteran summed up American exceptionalism succinctly when he said that on America's worst day, he would rather live here than in any other country in the world. This is a veteran whose long career in the military took him to numerous countries around the world. He saw firsthand what it's like to live outside the United States. The same cannot be said for perennially pessimistic "elites" who take the good aspects of America for granted while focusing solely on the aspects in need of improvement.

What Makes Americans Willing to Go in Harm's Way for Our Country?

America was born out of the Revolutionary War ignited in 1775. Since that time, Americans have responded to our nation's call in the same way the Prophet Isaiah responded to the Lord's call when he said, "Here I am! Send me" (Isaiah 6:8). American citizens have donned the uniform many times to defend our nation and its allies from the forces of tyranny and evil. America exists in a dangerous world, one that due to international terrorism and a rising tide of aggressive behavior from countries such as China, North Korea, Russia, and Iran may be even more dangerous now than it has ever been.

Consequently, it is critical not just to our national defense but to our very survival as a nation that American citizens remain willing to put their lives on the line as Soldiers, Sailors, Airmen, Guardsmen, and Marines. We are concerned that if America strays too far from its moral roots and core values, there may come a day when our citizens are no longer willing to join the military to defend our country. This concern raises an interesting question those who reject America's moral roots and core values would do well to consider:

What makes Americans willing to put their lives on the line for our country?

Although this is a simple question, it has profound ramifications for America's long-term future. It's a question we have pondered and have asked many former and active-duty warriors over the years. Their answers have varied, but in the end they all boil down to the same thing: love of country. Americans are willing to fight and die defending the United States because they love our country. They love what America means to them as well as what it stands for in the community of nations.

This fact brings to mind the adage "America is great because she is good." This statement is often attributed to Alexis de Tocqueville, but in fact he never said it. Scholars still debate the statement's origins. Nevertheless, the contention is accurate regardless of its origin. It follows, then, that if America ceases to be good, America will cease to be great. It is this possibility that concerns most of the veterans we interviewed and surveyed in developing this book.

If love of country is what makes Americans willing to defend their country in uniform, what happens when the things Americans love about our country—its moral foundation and core values—are eroded beyond the breaking point? What happens when America ceases to be good in the eyes of Americans? At that point, it will also cease to be great. But this may not be the worst of it. If our country continues to travel down the road mapped out for it by progressives, the America we have known all our lives and studied in history books before they were revised could cease to exist—period. Many of the veterans we surveyed and interviewed fear this possibility.

Note About Our Veterans

The title of this book contains the question "Is this the America we fought for?" We wish to make an important point before proceeding. Not all military personnel fight in combat. Consequently, not all veterans are combat veterans. All branches of the military consist of two basic elements: the combat arms and the support troops. We believe all those who served in any capacity in the military—combat or support—fought for our country. This is because every job in the military, whether in combat or in a support billet, contributes in an important way to our national defense. The military doesn't just make up jobs. Every job in every branch of the military contributes in some way to our national defense.

For every warrior who carries a rifle, drives a tank, fires artillery, or flies a jet in combat, there must be support troops to prepare, assist, and care for that individual and the equipment. Without these support troops, those who go in harm's way would enter battle untrained, without effective planning, improperly equipped, poorly armed, and left on their own when wounded. Some of the veterans we surveyed and interviewed for this book served in combat and some served in support roles, but all served. This being the case, we believe they all fought in some capacity for our country.

President George W. Bush said it best during a tribute at Arlington National Cemetery on Veterans Day 2004:

> All who have served in this cause are liberators in the best tradition of America. Their actions have made our nation safer in a world full of new dangers. Their actions have also upheld the ideals of America's founding, which defines us still. Our nation values freedom—not just for ourselves, but for all. And because Americans are willing to serve and sacrifice for this cause, our nation remains the greatest force for good among all the nations on Earth.[1]

Note About Our Survey and Interviews

We surveyed and interviewed more than five hundred veterans in preparation for writing this book. However, we do not claim this to be a statistically representative sample of all veterans. Military veterans tend to be more conservative than the general population, but there are plenty of veterans at both ends of the political spectrum as well as in the middle. There are even veterans who are progressives. However, what we do claim is there are a lot of veterans concerned about the state of our nation. We know this to be true not just because of the survey and interviews we conducted, but also because we are constantly in touch with veterans from all over the country and have been for a long time.

A Veteran Speaks Out

"In today's world of globalism with ubiquitous access to informa-
tion, there is a definite increase in fringe actors jamming the true
message of what it means to be an American. The far left has been
increasing the signal strength of their jamming in an attempt to
destroy the core message of what America is and why we should love
and defend this great country. If we stand by and do not change
or challenge the frequency and power we are using to commu-
nicate, there is the potential for their effectiveness to increase. If
that happens, then they will have been successful in stripping us of
our love of country and our willingness to fight for our nation on
foreign battlefields."

—*MAJOR GENERAL (RETIRED) JEFFREY R. RIEMER,*
U.S. Air Force, 1974–2008

General Riemer served his country for thirty-four years,
beginning his Air Force career as a fighter pilot in F-4C
Wild Weasels. He spent the rest of his career as a test
pilot, flying more than forty different kinds of aircraft
including the X-29. Riemer was the top graduate of his
pilot training, instructor training, and test-pilot school
classes. He is a recipient of the Air Force Institute of
Technology's Distinguished Alumni Award.

Over the years, we have talked with thousands of veterans,
former warriors who have shared their concerns about the state
of our nation. The concerns expressed in these conversations
mirror the results of our survey and interviews for this book.

If the veterans we have talked with over the years and surveyed have these concerns, so do many other veterans we have not talked with. Further, we believe that because they sacrificed to serve our nation, veterans and the views they express should be given due consideration by Americans of all stripes.

The issues chosen for inclusion in this book, as listed in the table of contents, are those the veterans surveyed and interviewed rated highest on a scale of one to five, with one indicating "Not Concerned" and five indicating "Very Concerned." All issues chosen for inclusion in this book had an average score for all respondents of 4.6 or higher. Some of the issues in the survey were so closely related that we combined them into one chapter (for instance, porous borders and sanctuary cities). Because the survey guaranteed the respondents' privacy and anonymity, veterans who completed it were candid in stating their opinions in the comments section. Some of their comments are summarized and paraphrased throughout this book.

A Veteran Speaks Out

"I think I have a good grasp of what progressives are trying to do to our country, but for the life of me I cannot believe they have a true vision of what their final outcome would be."

—Michael A. Fregger, O.D., U.S. Army, 1979–1985

Dr. Fregger is past president of the Florida Optometric Association and is now a physician in private practice.

Call to Action for All Americans

We wrote this book as a wake-up call to action for all Americans. Securing the future of America is not a liberal-versus-conservative or Democrat-versus-Republican issue. It is an issue for all Americans. Our purpose in writing this book is to encourage citizens of all worldviews and political persuasions to become good stewards of America's future. To be a good steward in the current context means to pass our country on to the next generation in better condition than it was when we inherited it. Americans of all stripes and political and religious affiliations are responsible for determining what America's future will be. We are all called to be good stewards of those things that made America great and a nation worth fighting for.

We hope after reading this book, Americans on the left, in the middle, and on the right will step back and consider the long-term consequences of their short-term actions. The future of America is more important than short-term personal gain or political power. Americans of all political persuasions and worldviews need to set their sights farther down the road than the next election and start considering what they want America to be, not just for them but for their grandchildren, great-grandchildren, and great-great-grandchildren. As citizens of a free and self-governed nation, we have it in our power to write a bright future for America or to pen its obituary.

Unless we want to spend our golden years apologizing to our grandchildren for squandering their national inheritance, Americans of all stripes need to put aside self-serving agendas and work together to rebuild a moral foundation that, although showing cracks, can still be restored to a condition that guarantees a brighter future for all Americans for generations to come. We think it is time for Americans who believe in what our country stands for to stand and speak out for those things.

Few moments in our nation's history reflect a greater need for such righteous action than the divisive times we now endure. Certainly, the eight-year-long American Revolution was one. So too was our bitter, bloody Civil War. Both these vicious, sanguinary contests pitted Americans against one another. And each had elements similar to current events.

Our 1775–1783 fight for independence was nearly doomed by what we now call a pandemic. Back then it was smallpox. So too, our Civil War—rife with deadly pestilence, disease, and infection—resulted in more of our countrymen killed, wounded, and disabled than all our other military conflicts combined.

Not one of the veterans we interviewed for this work condone any American being denied equal opportunity for "life, liberty, and pursuit of happiness." None of us want anyone to be the target of unlawful behavior by those responsible for enforcing our laws.

Nor should law-abiding Americans be subjected to wanton barbarity by vandals wreaking anarchy with looting, arson, and abhorrent threats to life and limb. We, the authors—and all others in this book—took an oath "to support and defend the Constitution of the United States..."—all of it—for all Americans.

And we also know for certain the toxic result of government enforced "quarantines"; arbitrary decisions by "government officials" on what "businesses" can remain open; whether we are allowed to go to church, or keep a job while foreign and domestic adversaries threaten our nation's security and economy.

Our hope and prayer is this book will encourage all who read it to join the battle of ideas currently raging in our country and to fight the good fight on behalf of what makes our country worth fighting for.

Psalm 91 is our refuge. Romans 8:28 inspires us. Both are Truth!

CHAPTER 1

Growing Acceptance
of Socialism

The premise: "The misguided preference for socialism is more of a systemic problem than a generational problem. While it is easy to blame the obliviousness of college students these days, perhaps we should look at how they evolved into this grave level of ignorance. Teachers' unions and tenured professors have 'taught' this generation that capitalism is exclusive and racist while socialism is inclusive and accepting. This, coupled with misguided parenting, has led an entire generation to be blissfully ignorant about right and wrong and, in turn, the notion of responsibility. With 20 percent of millennial adults choosing to live at home with their moms and dads, we will not succeed in re-educating that generation, because their teachers, parents, and society are enablers. The current college-age generation seems to have little or no respect for the military, yet they have no idea what we have done for them and continue to do for them. We are swimming in a sea of ignorance and mediocrity. If things don't change, we will drown in it."

—BRIAN HAUGEN, *U.S. Army Special Forces, 1986–2008*

The veteran who expresses the premise for this chapter is Lieutenant Colonel (retired) Brian Haugen. Colonel Haugen served our country for twenty-three years as an Army Ranger and member of the Army's elite Special Forces. He was commissioned in 1986 through the Reserve Officers Training Corps (ROTC) at Marion Military Institute. His commissioning was followed by duties including service as an Airborne Platoon Leader, Battalion Support Company Commander, Group Support Company Commander (20th Special Forces Group—Airborne), and Chief of the Joint Operations Center (Combined Joint Special Operations Task Force in Bagram, Afghanistan).

Colonel Haugen's military commendations and decorations include the Combat Infantry Badge, Master Parachutist Badge, Honduran Jumpmaster Wings, German Parachute Badge, Meritorious Service Medal, Joint Services Commendation Medal, Army Commendation Medal with one oak leaf cluster, Army Achievement Medal, Southwest Asia Service Medal with one star device, Army Meritorious Unit Citation (Desert Shield), Global War on Terrorism Expeditionary Medal, Afghanistan Campaign Medal, and Liberation of Kuwait Medals (Saudi Arabia and Kuwait). As a civilian, Haugen has built a successful career in business as a certified financial advisor.

Socialism is Becoming More Popular

Our featured veteran for this chapter, Haugen, makes an important point about the growing acceptance of socialism, particularly by people of college age. Parents, teachers, and society in general are all complicit in this travesty by failing to educate young people and by accepting mediocrity instead of encouraging excellence. Many young people of today have been raised in unprecedented affluence, a condition they take for granted.

Even people who qualify as poor by today's standards have air conditioning, automobiles, cell phones, and microwave ovens. Young people shop in stores overflowing with items from all over the world. They can buy fruits and vegetables year-round people from earlier generations didn't know even existed. Unfortunately, the young people of today take their affluence for granted and do not realize it hasn't always been this way. For example, most of the veterans interviewed for this book grew up without air conditioning. Our lives of abundance in the United States exist because of capitalism. Even with its acknowledged imperfections, capitalism is far better than any other economic philosophy ever imagined.

Affluent living with no appreciation of how things used to be can take a toll on young people, making them soft physically, mentally, and morally. One of the veterans interviewed for this book opined that rather than raising the next generation of intrepid explorers willing to risk everything to go to the moon and beyond, we have raised a generation of snowflakes who think adversity means being without a cell phone for thirty minutes. This veteran wondered what would happen to our country if we had to rely on snowflakes to protect us from the hardened tyrants of the world.

No aspect of America's character is under more persistent attack from the left than Christianity. Sir Winston Churchill once pointed out an interesting distinction between Christianity and socialism. This distinction is important because some socialism advocates claim their philosophy is just the second part of the "greatest commandment" put into action. They claim socialism means loving your neighbor as yourself. Churchill refuted this claim when he pointed out Christians give voluntarily to neighbors in need in accordance with the teachings of Christ, while citizens of socialist countries are forced to give through government coercion whether they want to or not.[2]

This comparison demonstrates in just a few words one of the most fundamental flaws of this ignorant philosophy. Nevertheless, in spite of having a track record worse than a three-legged greyhound, socialism is becoming all the rage among younger Americans. Young people in America who have never lived in a socialist country and, therefore, have never experienced socialism firsthand are now claiming they prefer it to capitalism. Opinions based on a lack of knowledge are dangerous.

In a recent Gallup poll, 43 percent of respondents indicated they viewed socialism favorably. A similar poll taken in 2017 by the Victims of Communism Memorial Foundation revealed 44 percent of Americans between the ages of twenty-one and thirty-six favor socialism over capitalism. This is the age cohort often referred to as millennials. Encouraged by unrealistic promises made by leftist politicians and the false teachings of college professors, young people in America are adopting socialism as their economic philosophy of choice. This is hardly surprising when its advocates promise them free healthcare, free college, and student-debt forgiveness.

To college graduates carrying a heavy burden of student debt while working in jobs they could have gotten with just a high school diploma, promises of debt forgiveness must sound enticing. To their counterparts about to start college, free college must sound equally enticing. Add promises of free healthcare and you will easily hook the economically illiterate among us. What is especially disappointing about this everything-should-be-free mentality is that college students have no qualms about running up huge amounts of debt and then expecting others to pay their debts. The others who will eventually pay are you and me.

On a side note within this context, why does no one seem to have a problem with college higher-ups living pampered lives financed by the high tuitions they charge, which result in the debt burden carried by students? If you look carefully at this, you'll see the socialist model at work: a few living high off the hog of cultural ignorance.

A Veteran Speaks Out

"It's not just college students who claim they prefer a socialist economy. It's also people in the mid to lower income brackets. In the early 1990s, I was stationed in the Netherlands, where their income was taxed at approximately forty-six percent. They had one doctor for a large area, and everyone, including babies and the elderly, had to go through this doctor in order to get a referral to another doctor. Most people lived in small high-rise apartments, and few owned vehicles due to the high cost of getting a license. There is no incentive to work hard if the government is going to take almost half of your money."

—MISTY LEE FENTON, U.S. Air Force, 1982–2003

Fenton served in logistics in the Air Force for twenty-one years. While serving in the Air Force, she earned an associate degree and a bachelor's degree. Following her retirement from the Air Force, she earned a master's degree in counseling and development. She is currently in private practice providing cognitive behavioral therapy and accelerated resolution therapy.

But there is a problem with asking you and me to pay off the student loans of young people we've never even met. We didn't borrow the money, and it is not our college education that put them in debt. It's their education, for what it's worth, and their debt. Why should you and I pay for it? Further, if we forgive millennials their student debt, why stop there? Why not let them borrow money to buy a house and a car, and then ask others to pay off those debts? Why not let them run up credit-card debt and then ask others to pay off the banks?

One of the veterans interviewed for this book said he never had an opportunity to go to college, because he had to work hard all of his life to support his family and the family of a brother who was killed in Vietnam. He wanted to know why he should be asked to pay the debts of students who had been blessed with the opportunity to go to college when he hadn't been. Good question. Promises of free this and that resonate with millennials because they are accustomed to others paying their way. Now they want you and me to pay their way.

Until millennials were college aged, Mom and Dad paid for everything. In college, student loans guaranteed by the federal government paid the bills. Now, as college graduates, they are coming face-to-face with the harsh reality of what it means to borrow money irresponsibly and are looking for a convenient way out. Forgiving their student debt—which just means forcing others to pay for it—will only reinforce and reward their irresponsible behavior. This, in turn, will just encourage more irresponsible behavior on their part, because when you reward any kind of human behavior, you get more of that behavior. If you want less of a given behavior, don't reward it.

Of course, had young Americans buying into the false promises of socialism been educated rather than indoctrinated, they would know nothing is free. Somebody has to pay. Another lesson they might have learned had college taught them to be critical thinkers instead of just the opposite is this: Anything that sounds too good to be true probably is. Socialism is one of those concepts that sounds good in theory but never pans out in reality. Why? Because it fails to take into account human nature, and human nature is the Achilles heel of socialism.

"Socialism" Defined

One of the problems you run into when talking with advocates of socialism is many of them don't really know what it is. Further, having never lived in a socialist country, they have no idea of how life would be in a socialist system. Every semester, one of us asks students in his college classes to define socialism. Typically, the best they can do is state that socialism means everything is free. If only life were that easy. Socialism is an economic philosophy in which the government owns and administers the means of production and distribution of goods and services. Socialism is a command economic system as opposed to a demand system. Understanding the difference is critical.

With socialism, there is central planning by government bureaucrats to determine what will be produced and in what quantities. In other words, the government decides what you need and commands it be produced by government-operated organizations. With capitalism, you—the consumer—decide what will be produced and in what quantities. An economist calls this demand. In a free-market economy, private-sector businesses survive by providing you—the consumer—with what you demand. They thrive by satisfying your demands in the right amounts, at the right price, and at an acceptable level of quality. Unlike government-owned and -operated organizations, private-sector businesses must compete to survive. They aren't like the post office, for example, which can simply raise the price of stamps every time inefficiency threatens to bring insolvency.

Don't just gloss over the definition of "socialism"; think about it. How would your life change if all of the businesses you interact with were owned and operated by the federal government? For example, have you had the experience of waiting in long lines at the post office? Have you had to put your name on a mile-long waiting list at a Veterans Administration (VA) clinic? Have you had to take a number and stand in line at a Social Security office?

There is a reason Federal Express, United Parcel Service (UPS), and other delivery businesses are prospering. There is also a reason the federal government had to start sending veterans to private healthcare facilities to cut down on the number waiting to be treated at VA hospitals. There is a reason trips to government offices can be so frustrating. The reason in all of these cases is the same: inefficiency, a weakness intrinsic to government organizations. The lack of competition and accountability in government breeds complacency and stifling bureaucracy.

Private-sector businesses are more efficient, more eager to please, and easier to work with because if you aren't satisfied with their products or services, you can take your business elsewhere. If you get poor service from a clerk at one store, no problem; go to another. If you can't find the books you need in your local bookstore, no problem; shop online. But when dealing with the government, there is nowhere else to go when you are unhappy with the service. Tired of waiting in long lines at the Social Security office? Too bad. There is nowhere else you can go. Governments are monopolies, and monopolies don't have to worry about whether you are satisfied with their products or services. Worse yet, they can charge anything they want for their products and services.

Socialism creates the ultimate monopoly. In a socialist economy, you have to depend on the federal government for almost every product or service you need, which is why there is always a thriving black market in socialist countries. With central planning, what you need might not even be available. However, if you get lucky and it is, you still have to find ways to convince bored, unmotivated bureaucrats why they should serve you instead of the hundreds of other people waiting in line for the same thing you want. This is why bribery is so prevalent in socialist countries, and bribery is why socialist bureaucrats are often better off financially than everyday citizens in those countries.

Then, even if you are able to convince the bureaucrat in question to serve you, there is still a major obstacle to be confronted. You have to hope central planners in the federal government guessed right when they decided how many of the products in question would be needed. Rather than base their estimates on consumer demand, they typically just depend on how many were produced the previous year, an approach that fails to account for changes in demand. This is why chronic shortages are an everyday part of life in socialist countries. To put this aspect of socialism into perspective, try to imagine what would happen if bureaucrats in Washington, D.C., ran Walmart.

The inherent shortcomings of central planning and its resultant shortages are the origin of a joke that used to circulate about the Soviet Union before its socialist economy crashed and burned. A veteran in our survey reminded us of this joke. A Muscovite has been on a waiting list for three years to purchase a car, a commodity always in short supply in the Soviet Union. When the government-operated car dealer finally calls him to say he has a delivery date, the Muscovite quickly grabs his appointment book so he can block out the day. The car dealer tells him, "Your car will be delivered at twelve noon on June second two years from now." Expecting his customer to be delighted, the car dealer is surprised to hear only silence on the phone line. Finally, with resignation born of experience, the Muscovite says, "I can't pick the car up on that day. That's when the plumber is coming."

Why Do Progressives Reject the America of Our Founders?

One of the veterans from our survey asked a pertinent question. He wanted to know why the progressives of today reject the America envisioned by our founders. Why are they so determined to change what has worked so well for so long? The answer to his inquiry is simple but disturbing. Progressives know their vision of big government is incompatible with the vision of limited government advocated by Americans who share the vision of the founders. Progressives worship at the altar of government control. This is why they put so much effort into tearing down the church and family. They want full control of the lives of Americans without the inconvenience of competition.

At this point, we will begin using a more appropriate term for these anti-Americans. If the presidency of Donald Trump has accomplished nothing else (and it has accomplished a great deal), it has forced those trying to hide behind a seemingly innocuous label to confess who they are: socialists. Plaster any label you'd like over it, but anyone who wants governmental dominance is a socialist.

The founders' vision of a nation built on Christian principles is anathema to socialists, who want to use the government to control every aspect of your life. The founders envisioned an America in which power resided in the people in the broadest sense. Socialists envision an America in which power resides in just a few people: them. The "progressive" (read: socialist) agenda in America can be summarized as follows:

Step 1: Government controls the people.

Step 2: Socialists control the government.

Step 3: Socialists control the people.

This three-step proposition explains why socialists are so intent on driving God out of every aspect of American life while also suppressing traditional American institutions such as the church and family. Americans who put the God of Holy Scripture first in their lives and put family a close second will never accept government as the center of their universe. This same proposition explains why socialists are doing everything they can to encourage illegal immigration into our country.

The immigrants illegally flooding our southern border are not coming here because of America's Christian heritage and traditional core values, or even for opportunity, as was the case with the earlier waves of immigrants who entered through Ellis Island. They are coming here to be taken care of by the federal government. They want America's government to do what their governments promised but couldn't do: take care of them. Socialized medicine and monthly welfare payments don't appeal to people who share the founders' vision for America, but to immigrants from some of the world's poorest socialist countries, the United States represents a government-financed paradise.

Socialists understand this. It's why they view illegal immigrants not just as future voters for their candidates but as voters who can be easily manipulated because they dine at the public trough. One of the veterans in our survey commented that socialists are willing to see America crash and burn in order to gain political power, but they don't have the good sense to know that when the roof of the house falls in, it will fall on them too. This veteran is right. The sad truth is that socialists are willing to throw America under the bus in order to gain political power, but if they get their way, the America of today will be the Venezuela of tomorrow and socialists will find themselves under something much worse than a bus, just like the rest of us.

Some Straight Talk for Millennials About Socialism

It is easy to become frustrated with young people who turn to socialism without a thought for, much less an appreciation of, how their lives have been blessed by capitalism. However, rather than become frustrated, we recommend educating young people about the inherent shortcomings of socialism. After all, as our featured veteran for this chapter commented, young people who buy into the supposed promise of socialism are just parroting, in most cases, what they have been taught in grade school and college.

The leftist indoctrination so prevalent in schools, colleges, and textbooks these days led one veteran who responded to our survey to say he decided to stop paying his grandson's college tuition. This veteran said he had been sending his grandson to college to be educated, not indoctrinated. When the young man came home one weekend spouting socialist propaganda, the grandfather had heard enough. Having worked hard for years to build a better life for his family, this elderly veteran wasn't going to allow his grandson to take his money with one hand and slap him in the face with the other.

The utopian ideals of socialism taught in schools and colleges are little more than myths perpetuated by elitist teachers and professors who have never had to experience the harsh realities of the philosophy they advocate. Worse yet, they ignore the well-documented failings of socialism worldwide while attacking the moral foundation and core values of the country that has given them such good lives. Here are just a few points that should be understood by people who claim to prefer socialism to capitalism:

- Socialism eliminates private property. What is yours now—smart phone, laptop computer, car— would no longer be yours in a socialist country. It would belong to the government. Worse yet, your talent, ideas, and ingenuity would belong to the government. If you were to design an app for smart phones that earns millions of dollars, those dollars would go to the government, not you.

- The only things socialism has consistently delivered for over a century are more poverty for more people, government tyranny, an increase in want and unmet needs, an off-the-charts misery index, and a state of inequality in which the only winners are the bureaucrats who hold the strings of power. If leftist teachers and professors had a shred of intellectual integrity, they would require their students to study the lives of the citizens of North Korea—many of whom are starving to death; of Venezuela, where everyone who can leave the country is doing so; and of Cuba, where most citizens endure a hand-to-mouth existence and have for decades. If schools and colleges did what they are supposed to do—teach young people to think critically—instead of operating like the re-education camps of communist dictatorships, young people would reject socialism outright.

- Whereas the governments of capitalist democracies seek to protect the security and rights of individuals, the governments of socialist countries protect only the government. Individual rights are of no concern in a nation dedicated to collectivism. Socialism makes the government all-powerful and the individual insignificant. This invariably leads to abuses of power by government bureaucrats and, eventually, government tyranny. A veteran we talked with used an example from his days in the Army to make this point. On the issue of supplies needed by him and his fellow warriors, he stated the non-commissioned officer (NCO) in charge of the supply depot never seemed to go without the best of everything, even when he claimed the items the troops needed were out of stock. Another veteran, in commenting on this issue, put it even more plainly when he said that while serving in the Navy, he'd never met a skinny cook. Similarly, in a socialist country, it's the bureaucrats who prosper, not the people.

- In capitalist democracies, the individual reigns supreme. The Bill of Rights appended to the U.S. Constitution has one overriding purpose: protection of the individual citizen from the power of government tyranny. The founders were adamant that America's government not become like those of European countries ruled by all-powerful monarchs. In socialist countries, government bureaucrats reign supreme, while individuals have a right to only what the government decides they have a right to. In other words, in socialist countries, the individual is just one more cow in the herd.

- Socialism advocates like to claim they can deliver free everything for everyone. But "free everything" is one of the biggest lies ever perpetrated on a naive and ill-informed generation. It is estimated the socialist programs advocated by prominent socialists in the Democratic Party would cost more than forty trillion dollars ($40,000,000,000,000) to implement. Ironically, young people who claim to prefer socialism to capitalism are the ones who ultimately would get stuck paying the bill when higher taxes are imposed on everyone. Contrary to the claims of socialism advocates, the rich cannot be taxed enough to pay for what "free everything" would cost. In America, the rich and the middle class already do the heavy lifting when it comes to paying taxes, while those at the lower end of the socioeconomic spectrum pay little or none. A veteran who responded to our survey was appalled to learn that some Americans were receiving checks from the IRS for either not working or earning too little. He was incensed. According to this veteran, it's one thing to let people get by without paying taxes, and it's quite another to reward them with a check the rest of us have to pay for.

- An obvious problem with requiring the rich to pay for the lives others would live is when the government can end up taking too much of the wealth people have earned, and the wealthy won't simply sit back and passively go along with being robbed. Instead, they would respond in one of three ways. One way would be to leave and take their money with them. Another would be to simply stop doing the entrepreneurial and productive things that made them rich. Both of these responses would lead to massive unemployment, because entrepreneurs are the people who create jobs in a capitalist economy. That's how they become wealthy. A final potential response of the wealthy would be to get lawyered up and fight the government in the courts forever, which they could afford to do. The point is, the wealthy wouldn't simply sit back and passively accept the abuse of socialists in government. Never forget, people respond to incentives. Take away the incentives to be productive and entrepreneurial, and people will stop being productive and entrepreneurial or, more likely, they will relocate to countries where these actions are rewarded.

- Socialism emphasizes cooperation and discourages competition, entrepreneurship, and innovation. Cooperation means people work together for the good of the group. An economic system that depends on people consistently doing this is doomed from the outset. People don't always cooperate. They don't always do what they are supposed to do. Think of your fellow students when you were in school. Some students studied hard, did their homework, and were punctual in attendance, while others skipped school, partied instead of studying, and ignored assignments. Capitalism rewards the former and punishes the latter. Socialism ignores the former and tolerates the latter. Some people work hard and in a smart way, while others do just enough to get by. Again, capitalism rewards the former and punishes the latter. Socialism ignores the former and tolerates the latter. A veteran who responded to our survey commented on the idea that people are cooperative by nature. He claimed if this were true, the Army would not have needed NCOs like him. His most important job as an NCO was to apply appropriate pressure in appropriate ways to get soldiers to do what they were supposed to do in the first place. It's also why organizations, public and private, have supervisors and communities have police; people don't always do what they are supposed to.

- Socialism encourages inefficiency. Have you ever known a government bureaucracy to function more efficiently than a private-sector organization? The reason private organizations are typically more efficient and more customer-friendly is their employees are rewarded for efficiency. Government bureaucrats are not. In government, if you process ten forms per hour or just two, you are paid the same, so why work harder or smarter to be more efficient?

- Socialism encourages groupthink and conformity, which are the enemies of innovation and continual improvement. Innovation and continual improvement lead to growth and expansion. Groupthink and conformity lead to stagnation.

- A core principle of socialism is central planning of the economy. With capitalism you, the consumer, decide what you want and in what quantities. Businesses then respond accordingly. Businesses fulfilling your needs with quality products and services at reasonable prices in a timely manner succeed. Those that don't, fail. A key point here is businesses are constantly competing with one another to meet your needs in a better, faster, less expensive way. With capitalism, the customer rules, and you are the customer. With socialism, bureaucrats far removed from you and your needs rule. They decide what will be produced and in what quantities. You, the customer, have no voice in the matter. Whereas with capitalism the customer is always right, with socialism bureaucrats are always right, even though they are often wrong. The problems with central planning should be obvious. However, if they are not, just study the downfall of the former Soviet Union, life in Cuba, or what has happened in Venezuela.

An interesting conversation about socialism took place in a grocery store parking lot during the development of this book. A veteran-turned-college professor explained how he teaches the benefits of capitalism over socialism to his political science students. When the time comes for the midterm exam each semester, just before handing out the tests, this professor tells his students they have to choose between a capitalist and a socialist grading system.

With the socialist system, he will tally the test scores and compute the class average. Everyone in class will receive the class average, usually a C, as their grade. Even those who otherwise would have received an A, B, D, or F, will receive a C. There will be no extra-credit questions for improving test scores. With the capitalist system, all students will receive the grade they earn, and there will be an extra-credit essay question so those students who have studied hard can have a chance to improve their scores.

According to this veteran-turned-professor, he has yet to have a class choose the socialist grading system. College students, including those who claim to prefer socialism over capitalism, guard their grade-point averages jealously. Many plan to attend graduate school and know they will need a good GPA to be accepted. There are always a few who vote for the socialist system, but those are the students who have skipped class, are behind on homework assignments, and have failed weekly tests. In other words, they are already failing the class, so a C on the midterm would be an improvement for them. The professor's lesson makes an important point about socialism we've already stated several times: It rewards counterproductive behavior while failing to reward efficiency, productivity, and entrepreneurship.

A Veteran Speaks Out

"The advice I would give college students who are thinking about going into debt with student loans is the same advice I gave my soldiers before releasing them on a weekend: Have a plan. In addition to the students who naively take out large student loans, blame must also fall on the issuers of the debt. If they release loans without nailing down accountability measures that show the debt is being used to ensure future success in a field that will allow the debt to be repaid, they need to talk with students about expectations."

—PATRICK BYRNE, *U.S. Army, 2006–2015*

Byrne served as company commander, Headquarters and Headquarter Company, 2nd Battalion, 501st Parachute Infantry Regiment, 4th Airborne Brigade Combat Team, 82nd Airborne Division.

Socialism Is Like Ice Cream

Socialism comes in a lot of different flavors and looks good, but it is bad for you if it's the center of your diet. The different flavors of socialism include revolutionary, democratic, libertarian, Fabian, market, green, and utopian socialism. Don't bother looking up the minor differences among these various approaches to socialism. They are irrelevant. Just as ice cream, no matter what flavor it happens to be, is essentially fat and sugar, the different kinds of socialism are essentially government control and coercion. Just as a steady diet of ice cream can ruin your health, socialism can ruin your ambition, initiative, drive, competitive spirit, work ethic, and entrepreneurial attitude.

On paper, socialism's utopian promises of equality, fairness, prosperity, security, and free this and that, can seem as appealing as ice cream on a hot day, but just as you should read the nutrition label before indulging in ice cream, you should look a little closer before accepting socialism. The "nutrition label" for socialism may be found by studying North Korea, Venezuela, Cuba, Nicaragua, and the former Soviet Union.

Refuting the Myth of Nordic Socialism

For those not blind to the failures of socialism, countries such as the former Soviet Union, Cuba, Venezuela, North Korea, and Nicaragua provide ample evidence that socialism doesn't work. Die-hard advocates of socialism, on the other hand, counter by pointing out the supposed success of socialism in Norway, Denmark, and Sweden. But the success of Nordic socialism is a myth. In his landmark book *Debunking Utopia: Exposing the Myth of Nordic Socialism*, Nima Sanandaji, who grew up in Sweden and holds a Ph.D. from that nation's Royal Institute of Technology, refutes five myths often repeated by advocates of socialism:[3]

1. *Denmark is an example of where socialism works.*
   Granted, Denmark's citizens are highly taxed and
   a high level of welfare is provided. But Denmark is
   not a socialist country with central planning and
   complete government control of the economy. Quite
   the contrary. Denmark has a market economy and
   ranks close to the United States in economic freedom.
   This is why it is able to fund the high level of welfare
   it provides its citizens. Its market economy works so
   well, it can afford the high level of welfare the government
   provides.

2. *Sweden became a wealthy nation by adopting socialism.* Capitalism was established in Sweden in 1870 and remained in force until 1936, when the social democrats came into power. During this period, Sweden's economy prospered. It wasn't until 1970 that social democrats tried to introduce socialist central planning. As a result, Sweden's economy began to falter. When a new government was finally elected in 1991, it moved the country back toward free markets, as have subsequent governments since that time. The result of this move back to free markets has been the prospering economy advocates of socialism find so attractive, a prosperity grounded not in socialism but in capitalism.

3. *Nordic welfare has produced positive results.* Citizens of Nordic countries do enjoy comparatively long life spans and a low child mortality rate. But those who attribute this admirable condition to socialism ignore an irrefutable fact: These positive outcomes existed before the welfare state was established. Consequently, they must be attributed to other factors relating to lifestyle rather than socialism.

4. *Nordic countries provide income equality.* Advocates of socialism attribute the relative income equality that exists in Nordic countries to government redistribution. However, once again, this is a misconception. Income equality was a reality in Nordic countries before the welfare state came into existence. Economists in these countries attribute the income equality to a Lutheran culture that emphasizes hard work and individual responsibility or, said another way, the Christian work ethic. The Christian work ethic is the polar opposite of socialism.

5. *Americans would benefit from adopting Nordic welfare.*
   The aspects of Nordic countries that advocates of
   socialism find most attractive can be attributed to the
   Nordic work ethic and lifestyle, not the welfare state.
   This can be seen by the fact that Nordic citizens who
   immigrate to the United States do better economically than their cousins back in the old country, as
   well as most other immigrants. Their work ethic, not
   welfare, is responsible for their prosperity.

The Nordic countries are highly taxed, and their welfare
levels are high, but they do not have centrally planned socialist
economies. Rather, what makes them attractive to ill-informed
advocates of socialism can be attributed to capitalistic factors: a
positive work ethic and market economies. In fact, it is a tribute
to free markets that Nordic countries can sustain themselves
while providing high levels of welfare and requiring high levels
of taxation. The Nordic countries are like wealthy people who
can absorb some bad investments simply because they have
enough money to take the loss.

Human Nature: The Achilles Heel of Socialism

One of the veterans who responded to our survey commented
that the biggest problem with socialism is it doesn't work.
This is a simple but profound statement. In just a few words,
this veteran summarized the bottom-line argument against
socialism. Forget the theories about socialism that sound so
enticing in a sterile academic setting. The differences between
the real and the ideal of socialism are stark and undeniable.
Socialism is a fundamentally flawed concept because it ignores
a critical factor: human nature.

Humans are hardwired to respond to incentives. As a general rule, people will choose the course of action that seems to most readily serve their self-interests. People are not, as advocates of socialism claim, cooperative beings who look out for the group first and themselves second. This fact is why organizations spend millions of dollars every year promoting teamwork among their employees while enjoying only mixed results. Ironically, the most effective way to get people to put the team first is to make it worth their while by providing incentives.

Responding to incentives is part of the survival instinct God gave us. This is why the most effective motivational techniques are based on one simple principle: With people, you get more of what you reward and less of what you don't. This principle is why sports teams select Most Valuable Players and businesses name Employees of the Year. It's why in sports and business, those who perform best are paid the most. It's why businesses offer performance bonuses to those who excel in their jobs. If you want people to do something, provide the right incentives, then get out of the way. Properly incentivized people will run over you to achieve the goal in question.

Understanding the value of providing incentives is why schools once named high achievers to the dean's list and graduated them with honors. Of course, this was before schools and colleges were infected by the snowflake philosophy (that is, the idea that rewarding high-performing students might hurt the feelings of their less dedicated counterparts). This everyone-wins, everyone-gets-a-trophy, and nobody-gets-their-feelings-hurt philosophy is the antithesis of capitalism, but it fits like a glove with socialism. Capitalism rewards excellence while socialism rewards mediocrity, and mediocrity won't pass muster in a globally competitive world.

Incentives also affect the way businesses do business. Because of the profit-loss incentive, businesses hoping to survive and thrive must provide customers with superior value. Superior value is a combination of superior quality, superior price, and superior service. Businesses able to provide customers these three factors in the right balance will enjoy a prosperous future. Those failing in this regard will have no future, which is a powerful incentive to give customers the quality, cost, and service they want. Government-run enterprises, on the other hand, have no incentive to do the hard work of pleasing customers, a fact explained earlier in this chapter.

The reason capitalism works well, if imperfectly, is rather than ignore human nature, it harnesses human nature and uses it for good. Socialism expects people to cooperate and collaborate voluntarily out of a commitment to the greater good. Capitalism incentivizes cooperation, collaboration, and the other behaviors that lead to efficiency, effectiveness, continual improvement, entrepreneurship, and innovation. Socialism fails because it ignores human nature.

Veterans Administration Hospitals: The Reality of "Free" Healthcare

One of the veterans who responded to our survey offered his opinion that anyone who claims to want socialized healthcare should be required to seek treatment at a hospital or clinic run by the Veterans Administration. There are 146 of them to choose from. For years, VA facilities have struggled with long wait times, packed waiting rooms, high rates of preventable infections, bed sores, and preventable deaths. This is not to say the doctors, nurses, and technicians who work in VA facilities are incompetent or uncaring. There are exceptions, of course, but for the most part the VA employs solidly credentialed, well-trained, caring professionals who are doing the best they can in an impossible situation. They are like race car drivers. Even the best drivers cannot win with a faulty car.

A Veteran Speaks Out

"The socialized, or so-called single-payer, healthcare system delivers access that because of limited resources specifies who, what, when, where, and how care is rendered. Given the history of the VA system, where veterans have been subjected to slow, limited, unresponsive, and unaccountable care, we should take warning about what that model of government-delivered, single-payer healthcare will look like. Care is only as good as its access and those who design and deliver it."

—*Donald Hamilton, M.D., U.S. Air Force, 1969–1996*

Dr. Hamilton served twenty-seven years in active and reserve duty. He began his Air Force career as a T-38 pilot, transitioned to medicine, and, along with his Air Force service, had a long and successful career in private practice as an otolaryngologist.

When the public outcry over veterans dying while waiting weeks and even months to be treated could no longer be ignored, elected officials were forced to act. Congress responded by doing what Congress always does when forced to act: It threw money at the problem and pressured a few high-level executives to resign. The biggest change was some veterans were allowed to seek treatment from private healthcare providers. In addition, other improvements were made, but for the most part the problems persisted. Why? Problems persist because VA hospitals operate according to the fundamentally flawed principles of socialized medicine. They come as close as anything you can find in America to pulling back the curtain and giving you a glimpse at what socialized medicine really looks like.

VA hospitals and clinics' being forced to send veterans to private healthcare providers proved an important point economists know well: Anytime their theories run up against the hard realities of life, socialists turn to capitalist solutions to rescue their sinking ships. Lenin had to do it after the communists ousted the czar and established the Soviet Union, Sweden had to do it after its unsuccessful foray into socialism, and VA healthcare providers are being forced to do it right now.

The decision allowing veterans to seek treatment from private healthcare providers has helped alleviate the problem of long waiting lines, but it has not solved the other problems associated with VA hospitals and clinics because these problems are too fundamental to be solved with mere stopgap measures. The sad truth is government healthcare providers will always suffer from bureaucratic inefficiency. Inefficiency is in the DNA of government organizations. The problems don't grow out of incompetence; they are systemic.

Because private hospitals and clinics must compete in a free-market environment, they have to provide high-quality healthcare in order to survive. Any private healthcare provider that earns a reputation for inefficiency, uncaring attitudes, poor record keeping, and preventable deaths will eventually fail. But

VA facilities—some of which have this kind of reputation—don't have to worry about going out of business. Government funding continues to flow regardless of what patients think, just as it does in socialized-medicine settings.

Granted, once the problems at VA hospitals and clinics garnered enough bad publicity, Congress got involved and a few heads rolled. But Congress and the media have the attention span of a hyperactive five-year-old. As soon as the headlines settled down, Congress moved on to more urgent problems, meaning those getting the most media coverage at the moment. Consequently, the fundamental flaws of socialized medicine persist, and those who depend on VA facilities for healthcare continue to experience problems.

One More Thought About Socialism

When history, experience, facts, and common sense paint socialism advocates into a corner, they have a last-ditch way of trying to get out of their dilemma. Their argument of last resort is the car-and-driver analogy. When the undeniable failings of socialism can no longer be denied, advocates like to claim the car is sound but has never had a competent driver. In other words, socialism is a legitimate economic philosophy that would work if only properly implemented by people who know what they are doing. The former Soviet Union, their argument goes, made a mess of socialism, but that was because the Soviet leaders were incompetent. Never mind those same leaders put the first satellite into space.

Socialism has failed not because those who have tried it are incompetent, but because it is a fundamentally flawed concept even the most competent practitioners could not successfully implement. In actual practice, socialism destroys individual initiative, entrepreneurship, and ambition while encouraging and even rewarding corruption. Ultimately it leads to misery, violence, tyranny, and kleptocracy. A kleptocracy is a government in which those who rule exploit the resources of their nation and steal from its citizens. For example, when Hugo Chavez of Venezuela died, he was worth $2 billion, all of it taken from the nation's oil resources and stolen from its citizens. At the same time as Chavez was becoming a bloated tyrant, the people of Venezuela were starving, eating domestic animals, and fighting over scraps in dumpsters. While Chavez became fabulously wealthy, medical doctors in Venezuela were earning little more than the equivalent of a dollar a day.

For socialism to work, the impossible goal of human perfection would have to be achieved. Socialists continue to believe, against all evidence, man can be perfected and paradise can be achieved in the here and now. A ten-year-old Sunday school student knows better. That issue was settled in the Garden of Eden. Perfection and paradise are characteristics of the hereafter, not the here and now.

Consequently, socialism does not work, will not work, and cannot work no matter how competent its practitioners may be. Granted, many who have sought to establish socialist economies were bad actors and some were incompetent. Think of Joseph Stalin, Fidel Castro, Mao Zedong, Hugo Chavez, and Pol Pot. But not all socialism advocates have been bad actors or incompetents. The Nordic leaders who experimented with socialism between 1970 and 1991 weren't bloodthirsty despots or fools. They were highly competent people with good intentions who wanted to do the right thing for their countries. Unfortunately, they chose the wrong car to drive in the big race, the global economic race. As a result, they had to admit their error and jump back into a car already proven worthy: capitalism.

A comment made by a veteran who responded to our survey contained a good suggestion. This veteran thought those who claim to prefer socialism over capitalism should be required to spend one year in Cuba, Venezuela, or some other bastion of socialism. Upon their return, they should be required to make a public report on what it was like. Comparing socialism advocates with city slickers who claim to be cowboys, this veteran made the point that they are all theory and no reality or, as they say in Texas, all hat and no cattle.

We will give Sir Winston Churchill the last word on socialism. Like most members of the British gentry, Churchill for many years was an outspoken advocate of paternalistic government. But after World War II, when he was no longer prime minister, Churchill had a front row seat to witness the results of actions taken by the political party that ousted him. During the years between 1945 and 1950, the Labour Party in Great Britain moved quickly to adopt the principles of socialism. It nationalized the Bank of England and essential services, including gas, coal, transportation, and trains.

Not surprisingly, these ill-advised actions resulted in record levels of taxation, shortages of essential commodities, higher prices, rationing, and a spike in the misery index. In a debate that took place in 1947, Churchill claimed that only if you set the people free to build better lives for themselves and their families can a successful property-owning democracy be established.[4] This was true in 1947 and it is true today, not just for Great Britain but for America too.

CHAPTER 2

Second Amendment Attacks

The premise: "*Our forefathers knew that those in power might become corrupt and seek to rule, just as the British eventually did by trying to disarm the colonists. It's not difficult to understand that a disarmed populace is a controlled populace. For this reason, it was crucial that the Second Amendment be included in the Bill of Rights. The ability to use firearms to defend one's family and country has been a hallmark of American freedom ever since. My fear is that today, as we move from fact-based to feelings-based decision-making, judicial activism, and ignoring the Constitution, it will be easy to blithely think getting rid of guns will get rid of suffering. Accordingly, there is no more important constitutional issue today than defending the plain language and original intent of the Second Amendment.*"

—*Erik Stoer, Ph.D., U.S. Air Force, 1973–2003*

*T*he veteran who expresses the premise for this chapter is Dr. Erik Stoer. Dr. Stoer is an Air Force veteran who served in uniform for thirty years, including his active-duty and reserve time. In addition, as a civilian, Dr. Stoer served in the Air Force for thirty-four years as a civil servant managing armament development projects. He served an additional eleven years as a defense contractor working in armament development. In addition to holding a Ph.D. from Florida State University, Dr. Stoer is a graduate of the Defense Systems Management College.

Make Progress or Just Make Noise: The Critical Choice

Dr. Stoer makes the important point that the gun-control debate is being driven by emotion and feelings rather than logic and reason. Gun control is a hot-button issue for socialists in America. The left's attacks on the Second Amendment are vitriolic, determined, and unrelenting. All too often, these attacks are long on emotion but short on reason. They tend to be more about government control than gun control. One of the veterans from our survey made the point that those who want to rescind the Second Amendment and confiscate legally owned guns are more concerned with controlling you and me than controlling guns.

This felicity about government control is ironic because, like the first eight amendments in the Bill of Rights, the Second Amendment is intended to protect you, the American citizen, from intrusive, coercive government. Further, the founders did not view the rights delineated in these first eight amendments as rights granted by the government. Rather, they viewed them as preexisting rights from God. Here is how the Second Amendment reads:

"A well regulated Militia being necessary to the security of a free state, the right of the people to keep and bear arms, shall not be infringed."

Socialists scoff at the contention that the Second Amendment protects individual gun owners from their own government. They like to ask, "How does having a handgun protect anyone from a government that has tanks and F-35s?" This argument is good for a cheap laugh but is disingenuous. People don't purchase handguns in anticipation of shooting it out with a tank or an F-35. They purchase handguns for recreational purposes and for protecting themselves and their families from home invasions. The Second Amendment protects from government intrusion individual gun owners who use guns in these lawful ways.

The Second Amendment is just one sentence, but it may be the most maligned, misunderstood, and misinterpreted sentence ever written. Its wording is clear, and founding documents explain the original intent of its authors. Why then does one plainly worded sentence generate so much consternation, controversy, and vitriol? We begin this chapter by answering this question because when it comes to responding to the never-ending gun-control proposals of the left, it is necessary to sort through a mountain of misinformation generated in support of a hidden agenda advanced by exploiting emotion.

A Veteran Speaks Out

"I can have an intelligent conversation with people who sincerely want to reduce gun violence but are prone to blame guns rather than the people who misuse them. They are just misguided and can be educated. But this isn't possible with those whose motivation is subtle and sinister, whose hidden agenda has nothing to do with reducing gun violence and who, in reality, don't even care if gun violence is reduced. These kinds of people have hardened hearts and no desire to know the truth. They blame guns rather than the people who misuse them because doing so suits their real purpose: achieving government control by a government they control."

—KENNETH GEIS, U.S. Army, 1979–1982

Geis is a firearms and firearm safety instructor certified by the National Rifle Association.

During the writing of this book, there were several high-profile mass shootings as well as violent attacks on police officers. The response of gun-control advocates was predictable: blame guns instead of the criminals who used them, capitalize on panic, whip up emotion, and exploit the grief of the victims' families. San Francisco officials even passed an ordinance labeling gun owners as domestic terrorists. Not only is this kind of response asinine; it is counterproductive. It does nothing to reduce gun violence in America.

If there is ever to be a productive, helpful dialogue leading to less gun violence in America, those who attack the Second

Amendment must decide if they want to make progress or just make noise. Vilifying law-abiding gun owners every time criminals misuse guns does nothing to reduce gun violence. Whipping up a frenzy of hand-wringing panic every time there is a mass shooting does nothing to reduce gun violence. Organizing antigun rallies in which lawful gun owners are demonized does nothing to curb gun violence. Finally, shamefully exploiting the grief of the families of victims does nothing to curb gun violence.

Americans who are sincere in their desire to curb gun violence must commit to doing the hard work necessary for progress rather than taking the easy route of making noise, pointing fingers, and placing blame. Reducing gun violence will require critical thinking on the part of the American public. It will also require socialists to put aside their hidden agendas and political posturing.

Those who use guns for criminal purposes pay no attention to existing laws. Consequently, it is certain they wouldn't honor the increasingly repressive laws that socialist gun-control advocates always recommend. Criminals don't obey laws; they break them. That's why we call them criminals. If it were somehow possible to take all the guns from every gun owner in America including criminals, within a week the criminals would be armed again. Only law-abiding citizens would be without guns. Gun-control laws do little more than ensure that people who already obey the law continue to do so while also rendering these law-abiding citizens more vulnerable to criminals who prey on society. That is not progress.

Self-Control Is the Most Effective Form of Gun Control

Those who attack the Second Amendment as well as those who defend it need to understand self-control is the only form of gun control ever to be effective. The adage "Guns don't kill; people do" is true. Guns are inanimate objects that do nothing until they are picked up and used by human beings. Those human beings decide how they are going to use guns. As one of the veterans in our survey said, guns don't control people; people control guns.

Therefore, the real issue is self-control, not gun control. This is why teaching, encouraging, and enforcing self-control is the only reliable solution to gun violence. Unfortunately, this is the opposite of what is happening in America. Parents, schools, and colleges have become so enamored of developing self-esteem they no longer teach self-discipline. Teaching young people self-control requires discipline, and "discipline" has become a bad word in the America of today. Hence, we have raised a generation of young people who think feeling like doing something is sufficient justification to actually do it, even if that means picking up a gun and killing as many people as possible. Past generations were taught to think before speaking or acting. The current generation is taught "If it feels good, do it."

Anyone who is serious about reducing gun violence must be willing to pursue solutions that go to the heart of the problem. We must be willing to objectively explore what has happened in America morally, socially, and culturally that would lead so many people to choose violence as their act of choice when they feel angry, frustrated, ignored, or marginalized. Progressive gun-control advocates are unwilling to do this because it is their misguided policies that have caused the degradation of behavior in America.

For example, because of policies championed by socialists, parents are now afraid to discipline their own children. If reported for spanking, parents can have their children taken from them by the state. Although spanking was a common form of discipline during our own school days and those of most of the veterans we interviewed for this book, no schoolteacher or administrator would dare spank a child in today's litigious environment. What used to be called discipline is now called abuse by socialists. The result of progressive policies is an undisciplined people lacking even a semblance of self-control acting out their anger in destructive ways. Many of them use guns.

Gun violence is a problem in America for two overlapping reasons: First, too many Americans have been raised on a diet of self-esteem rather than self-discipline, and self-expression rather than self-control. When young people brought up in this way become angry—no surprise here—they sometimes respond violently. Second, societal and cultural factors have eroded respect for human life. The root causes of gun violence in America are in us, not in guns. In other words, guns are not the problem; we are.

Lack of Self-Control and Lack of Respect for Life—a Dangerous Combination

There was a time in America when self-control was not just valued but expected. Just because you felt like doing something didn't mean you actually did it. Just because you felt like saying something didn't mean you actually said it. How many times in a fit of anger or frustration have you wanted to say or do something you might later regret? In answering this question, most people would say, "Many times." But in most cases you didn't do or say things you would have later regretted because you applied self-discipline and exerted self-control over your emotions.

When your coworkers make you angry, you don't take your gun to work and shoot them. In school, if classmates made you feel unwanted, you didn't steal an automatic weapon and try to wipe out the entire student body. With exceptions attributed to mental illness, those who commit gun violence choose to do so. They could just as easily choose not to by exerting the same kind of self-control you and millions of gun owners in America exert every day. The undeniable truth about gun violence is that the same gun in the hands of two different people is a completely different proposition. With one person it is a dangerous offensive weapon. With the other it is a safe defensive tool. The difference is in the person, not the gun. So, why do an increasing number of people fail to exert self-control and instead resort to violence? What has happened to self-control in America?

Parents, schools, churches, government, and society in general are complicit in the lack of self-control that leads an angry person to pick up a gun and use it in violent, destructive ways. American society is complicit because it has strayed from its Christians roots. Self-control is a biblical concept. In Proverbs 29:11 we read that "a fool gives full vent to his spirit, but a wise man quietly holds it back."

A Veteran Speaks Out

"God promised that the righteous would prosper, but America is turning its back on Him. The farther we stray from God, the worse things are going to get."

—WALTER WILLIAMS, *pastor, U.S. Air Force, 1970–1996*

Pastor Williams left the Air Force as a senior NCO. As a civilian, he has served in the ministry for more than twenty-five years.

Ironically, socialists who lobby unrelentingly for gun control are the same people who have driven God out of our schools, the public square, and government at all levels. Their anti-Christian policies are coming back to haunt them and all Americans in the form of gun violence. Sadly, the misery caused by gun violence is not limited to socialists whose misguided policies encourage it. All Americans suffer because of these regrettable actions and policies.

Churches are complicit because they have failed to use their grassroots influence to oppose the efforts of socialists to remove God from American life. All three branches of government are complicit because actions of the executive branch, Congress, and the judiciary over the years have eroded the authority of parents, teachers, coaches, school administrators, and even police officers to discipline young people during their formative years. Think back to July 2019 and the despicable instances of hoodlums pouring buckets of water on New York City police officers and taunting them while recording it all on smart phones. Since that time there have been numerous other instances of thugs openly harassing police officers while other citizens stood by and did nothing or, worse yet, applauded.

Schools are complicit because they have bought into the philosophy of the left that emphasizes self-esteem over self-discipline. Parents are complicit because they have allowed themselves to be hoodwinked by pseudo psychology that defines traditional disciplinary measures as child abuse in spite of the fact these measures worked well in raising generations of young people, including them. The most successful people in the history of our country grew up in a time when disciplining children was considered a parental responsibility, not child abuse.

Couple the lack of self-control with a lack of respect for human life, and you have a dangerous combination—one resulting in approximately forty thousand gun deaths every year. In times past, human life was considered sacrosanct. The worst crime a person could commit was murder, a crime prohibited by the Sixth Commandment. But constant exposure to gratuitous violence in movies, computer games, and on television has changed how a lot of people view human life. Is it any wonder people raised on a diet of gratuitous violence would come to view human life as cheap and expendable? Add to this that approximately seven hundred thousand unborn babies are legally murdered every year in America, and there is little doubt concerning why human life has lost its value in the eyes of many.

We believe a tipping point came with Darwin's disproven theory that humans are just another animal species. Though this godless concept of how man came to be on Earth has been repeatedly debunked, government schools continue to pour this lie into the minds of our kids. If your classmates are no different from the bug in your room, why not kill them if they bug you enough?

It is legal abortion more than anything else that prevents socialists from working to eliminate the root causes of gun violence in America. Abortion is the sine qua non of the American left. It is the untouchable plank in their political platform, the one coloring leftists' thinking on all other issues. If they were to admit abortion plays a role in the proliferation of gun violence, their whole house of cards would come crashing down, politically speaking. This is why socialists continually propose gun laws that will have no long-term effect on curbing gun violence. This kind of misdirection is what you do when you want to appear to be solving a problem. It's what you do when you are unwilling to admit the real cause of the problem is the policies advocated by the person you see when looking in a mirror.

Eliminating the Root Cause of Gun Violence

Any sophomore business major can tell you problems are solved by identifying and eliminating root causes. Gun violence would be reduced by changing human behavior, not changing gun laws. This contention is borne out by the fact only a tiny percentage of people who own guns ever use them to harm other human beings.

There are legally owned guns in approximately fifty million households in America, with the average being three guns per household, or 150 million guns total. According to Gun Owners of America Foundation (gunowners.com), gun violence accounts for approximately thirty-six thousand deaths per year in America. If guns rather than people killed, logic suggests this number would equal or exceed the number of guns owned in America. If this were the case, there would be 150 million or more deaths per year from guns. Victims of gun violence are wounded or killed not because of guns, but because people who lack self-control and have no respect for human life choose to use them in destructive ways (for example, to win arguments, rob and steal, settle debts, seek revenge, and so on).

If Americans are serious about reducing gun violence, we must be willing to put aside political correctness, posturing for political advantage, and exploiting the grief of the families of gun violence victims. Then we must focus on teaching young people to control themselves and value human life. Parents, teachers, elected officials, and the public at large all have a role to play in achieving this goal.

Restoring respect for human life and teaching self-control are the only approach that goes to the root cause of gun violence. Consequently, it is the only one that would effectively reduce gun violence. This being the case, one might reasonably ask: Why are socialists who are so vocal about reducing gun violence unwilling to even discuss this approach? One of the veterans from our survey answered this question when he commented that socialists are unwilling to talk about valuing human life because they don't value it, a contention borne out by their commitment to abortion. This veteran made the point that socialists love people in theory but not in practice.

When you are willing to kill innocent babies for the sake of convenience and then brush this atrocity off by labeling it "choice," valuing human life is not one of your favorite topics. Although they are loath to admit it, socialists who wring their hands over the thirty-six thousand deaths per year from gun violence have no reason to wonder why some people place little value on human life. Progressives can't have it both ways. They either value human life or they don't. It is hypocritical in the extreme to cry crocodile tears over the victims of gun violence while steadfastly defending abortion.

One of the veterans interviewed for this book told a story that demonstrates how much people have changed in America. When Jerry was in fourth grade, he and his classmates were required to participate in show-and-tell. Jerry brought his father's brand-new double-barrel shotgun to school for his show-and-tell project. He demonstrated how to make sure it was unloaded, how to clean it, and several safety measures for using it. The teacher was duly impressed and gave Jerry an A for his presentation. Two of Jerry's classmates also brought in guns for show-and-tell.

By way of contrast, Jerry commented on what would happen today if a student brought a double-barrel shotgun to class. The school would be put on lockdown, a SWAT team would be called, the fourth grader would be hauled off in hand-cuffs, and his parents would probably go to jail. Why is it a youngster could bring a gun to school in 1958 without anyone even raising an eyebrow, and yet today the same thing would cause a crisis big enough to make the national news? The answer is simple. Youngsters in 1958 could be trusted to handle guns without using them to hurt their classmates, because that's what they were taught. Parents, teachers, coaches, pastors, and the general public taught them to apply self-control and to value human life.

As socialists have pushed, pulled, and wrenched our country farther and farther from its Christian roots and tradi-tional values, there have been consequences. High on the list of consequences is the devaluation of human life coupled with a loss of self-control. This is a dangerous combination. As Jerry commented in his interview, socialists are just reaping what they have sown. Unfortunately, the rest of us are also reaping what socialists have sown. The left's dismissive attitudes toward Christian morality and traditional American values come at a price—a price we all pay.

Dispelling Gun-Control Myths of the Antigun Lobby

What can you do when you don't want to pursue the root cause of a problem and are promoting a plan you hope to keep hidden, but still want to appear as if you are taking action to solve the problem? If you are a progressive in America and the issue is gun control, you spin a web of misinformation and misdirection resulting in a series of gun-control myths, myths you know a cooperative mainstream media will repeat often enough the viewing audience will come to believe them. You may have heard the maxim that a lie repeated often enough becomes the truth. This statement is typically attributed to Adolf Hitler's right-hand man and chief propagandist, Joseph Goebbels. It's a favorite tactic of the left.

What follows in this section are some of the gun-control myths socialists have gone to great lengths to perpetuate. These myths are intended to make it appear to an American public concerned about gun violence that socialists are taking the lead in trying to solve the problem.

Myth Number 1: Gun-Free Zones Reduce Gun Violence

Claims of socialists notwithstanding, gun-free zones do not reduce gun violence. In fact, the opposite is true. The only thing gun-free zones accomplish is ensuring those who already obey the law continue to do so, as if they wouldn't anyway. The problem with the claim socialists make about gun-free zones is criminals don't care if an area is designated in this way. In fact, criminals are drawn to gun-free zones like moths to flames, because they know they will be the only ones there who are armed.

We are all safer when criminals know citizens are armed or even think they might be. All a gun-free zone accomplishes is making the world a more dangerous place for law-abiding citizens. Writing for *National Review*, John R. Lott Jr. makes the revealing point that since 1950, most of the mass shootings in the United States have occurred in locations where guns were prohibited. In Europe during this same period, every mass shooting without exception has occurred in a gun-free zone.[5]

Myth Number 2: Arming Citizens Does Not Deter Gun Violence or Save Lives

In his article for *National Review*, Lott mentions several instances in which criminals who were planning mass shootings were deterred because they feared armed opposition:

- James Holmes chose a movie theater in Aurora, Colorado, as a soft target and went on a rampage, killing twelve people and injuring seventy others. Holmes revealed in his diary that his original plan had been to attack an airport instead of a movie theater. He changed his mind because the airport had armed security guards and the movie theater didn't.

- In Conyers, Georgia, a man named Scott heard shots coming from a store. Two people in the store were killed. When Scott returned fire, the killer ran away. The local sheriff credited Scott, who had a concealed-carry permit, with saving the lives of the other customers in the store by scaring away the shooter.

- In Philadelphia, a man with a concealed-carry permit heard shots coming from a barbershop. Entering the shop, he spotted the assailant and shot him. The local police captain credited him with saving the lives of the others in the barbershop.

Lott's article in *National Review* gives numerous other examples of situations in which lives were saved and violence deterred because law-abiding citizens were armed. We won't belabor the point further except to reiterate that socialists are better at propagating gun-control myths than they are at doing anything that might actually curb gun violence.

Myth Number 3: Confiscating Guns Will Reduce Gun Violence

Socialists' theory—and that's all it is—seems to be that if you take away all the guns in America, there will be no more gun violence. But like so many theories that look good on paper but quickly break down in practice, this one has holes in it bigger than the Goodyear blimp. First, there is no way to confiscate all the guns in America. Even if you could force law-abiding citizens to give up their guns, you would still face the problem of convincing criminals to give up theirs, something any thinking person knows they won't do.

Second, if you could somehow magically confiscate all the guns in America—those of law-abiding citizens and those of criminals—within a week the criminals would be armed again. How? The black market and theft. Confiscating all guns would just create the kind of black market in America associated with drugs. Guns would flood into America from other countries right into the hands of criminals. Since law enforcement and military personnel would still be armed, theft of their weapons would skyrocket. Like most of the gun proposals advanced by socialists, this one would just leave criminals armed while leaving law-abiding citizens unarmed and at the mercy of the criminals.

Myth Number 4: Citizens Don't Need Guns to Protect Themselves

Socialists like to claim protecting the citizens of America is the job of the police and armed citizens are just self-styled vigilantes. One of the veterans from our survey pointed out the obvious fallacy in this contention. He commented that unless we are going to have one police officer for every citizen, there will always be times when the police cannot arrive in time to do anything but zip up the body bag. This is not to cast aspersions on the police, but, like most publicly funded enterprises, police departments are perennially underfunded and understaffed. Even when fully staffed, the police cannot be everywhere. There will always be more criminals than police. Consequently, it's a credit to their dedication and professionalism that police officers are able to do the outstanding job they typically do.

There are more than a million home invasions in America every year. Home invasions often involve robbery, rape, assault, and even murder. Then there is the growing problem of road rage. More than 65 percent of traffic fatalities are the result of aggressive driving, and more than 35 percent of road rage incidents involve firearms. In home invasions and road rage incidents, the damage from violent perpetrators is often done before the victims are able to call the police. The claim of socialists that citizens don't need guns to protect themselves is not just inaccurate; it's absurd.

Myth Number 5: Banning Automatic Rifles Would Reduce Gun Violence

One of the favorite tactics of socialists is to lobby for draconian gun-control measures using what they like to call "assault weapons" as the centerpiece of their argument. However, like many of their proposals, this one is based on misinformation and emotion rather than facts. Ignoring the fact "assault weapon" is a term invented by the media to promote a biased narrative, the fact is most gun deaths in America are caused by handguns.

The FBI compiles statistics on gun violence every year. The report from the FBI released during the development of this book showed that only 2 percent of gun-related homicides for that year were committed by people using rifles of any kind, including so-called assault rifles. More homicides were committed by people using knives (11 percent) than rifles. In fact, more homicides were committed by people using blunt instruments such as hammers and clubs or just hands, feet, and fists than using rifles of any kind.[6]

Labeling certain kinds of rifles "assault weapons" makes for good headlines, but in reality these kinds of weapons cause only a minuscule portion of gun deaths in this country. Ban this kind of weapon and the gun-violence meter would hardly budge. The antigun lobby would be better advised to ban hammers, clubs, fists, and feet than so-called assault rifles. But what socialists will do by banning certain types of rifles is ensure the only people who have these kinds of weapons are criminals on the streets of America.

Myth Number 6: Gun Ownership Is Not a Constitutional Right

The most ardent, devious, and manipulative gun-control advocates go directly to the source of your gun-ownership rights in an attempt to take them away from you. They claim that the Second Amendment does not give citizens the right to own firearms. We quoted the Second Amendment earlier in this chapter but quote it again here for the sake of convenience:

"A well regulated Militia, being necessary to the security of a free state, the right of the people to keep and bear arms, shall not be infringed."

Socialists who claim there is no right to gun ownership in the Second Amendment base their contention on the first four words of the amendment: "A well regulated Militia." They claim the intention of the founders was to allow private citizens to own guns so they could serve in local militias. Now that citizen militias have been replaced by the National Guard, civilian militias are no longer needed, or so say socialists. But the Supreme Court has ruled the Second Amendment does, in fact, give qualified adults the right to own and use guns for lawful purposes, and it specifically cites self-defense as one of those legitimate purposes (District of Columbia v. Heller, 554 U.S. 570, 2008).

How to Protect Your Second Amendment Rights

Although the Supreme Court has ruled you have a constitutionally guaranteed right to own guns and use them for lawful purposes, socialists have not stopped their attacks on the Second Amendment, nor will they. Consequently, it is important to stay on top of this issue and stay engaged in protecting the Second Amendment. What is legal today could be illegal tomorrow.

When it comes to the laws of the land in a constitutional republic, nothing is ever final. Ultimately, the laws of the land in America—including the Constitution—are what the Supreme Court decides they are. A change in the makeup of the court can result in a change in the laws of the land. The court's supposed allegiance to legal precedent notwithstanding, it does change its mind and it does overturn past rulings. This, of course, can be good or bad. It was good when it allowed America to take major steps forward in the civil rights movement. On the other hand, it could also lead to a new interpretation of the Second Amendment.

What all of this means to you is: 1) Never take your Second Amendment rights for granted; you can lose them, 2) vote for candidates for president and Congress, particularly for the Senate, who support the Second Amendment and will appoint and approve federal judges who support it, and 3) join at least one organization that supports the Second Amendment. This third recommendation is one of the most effective ways to guard your Second Amendment rights, because it multiplies your impact in the political arena by joining your time, money, and efforts with those of thousands of other Americans who share your concerns.

Organizations That Support the Second Amendment

There are numerous organizations in the United States dedicated to serving the needs of gun owners. Since the most important of these needs is to be able to legally own and use guns, the organizations listed below support the Second Amendment as part of their purpose.

1. National Rifle Association (NRA)

2. National Association for Gun Rights (NAGR)

3. Second Amendment Foundation (SAF)

4. United States Concealed Carry Association (USCCA)

5. Gun Owners of America (GOA)

6. Armed Citizens United (ACU)

7. Firearms Policy Coalition (FPC)

8. International Defensive Pistol Association (IDPA)

For specific information about these organizations, go to their websites. By supporting one or more of these organizations, you will be joining your voice with the voices of thousands of other gun owners who want to protect the Second Amendment and the right it gives Americans to own and lawfully use firearms.

CHAPTER 3
Historical Revisionism: Denying America's Christian Heritage

The premise: "Socialists have falsified history because they are in religious, philosophical, and ethical rebellion against God, the Bible, and Christianity as well as the foundations of American civilization, culture, civil government, and law. When they are called on this, they immediately resort to accusing others of 'hate speech.' But it's their policies and rhetoric that demonstrate hatred of anyone who opposes them, contempt for those they claim to want to help, and loathing of the beliefs, principles, and values that made America great. The policies of leftists take away individual freedom, encourage welfare, and produce countries that people eventually leave."

—ARCHIE JONES, PH.D., *U.S. Marine Corps, 1960–1964*

The veteran who expresses the premise for this chapter is Dr. Archie Jones. After serving his tour of duty in the U.S. Marine Corps and leaving the service as an NCO, he earned bachelor's, master's, and doctorate degrees. He became a Christian educator, college professor, and prolific author. Dr. Jones' books include *The Gateway to Liberty*, *Liberal Tyranny in Higher Education*, *Palin Nation*, and *Born to Lie* (a commentary on the lack of transparency in the Obama administration). He is currently coauthoring with his daughter, who is a professor of political science, a new book on the Christian foundations of the original state constitutions.

Why Socialists Are Revising America's History

Our featured veteran for this chapter, Dr. Jones, made an important point about those who revise and falsify America's history. He stated they are in rebellion. Socialists are rebelling against a history they must change in order to validate and justify their false narrative about America. The truth of history quickly reveals the falsehoods and half-truths in their narrative.

One of the authors had an interesting conversation on this subject with a stranger in an airport. A veteran, Victoria, was finally pursuing a degree in history after retiring from the Navy. She was concerned about professors who made a point of revising history to deny America's Christian heritage. Victoria revealed what had happened in one of her classes recently. The professor's lecture on the separation of church and state was not just biased; it was grossly inaccurate. When Victoria, who was well-read on the subject, attempted to set the record straight, the professor became incensed and loudly belittled her in front of the other students.

Victoria had been warned about this professor before enrolling in his class. The professor's anti-Christian bias was legendary throughout the student body. Comments about him on social media made it clear Christians who enrolled in his classes did so at their own risk. Even unbelievers in his classes were sometimes offended by this professor's vitriolic attacks on Christian students who had the audacity to suggest America's founders had been guided by Christian values. Consequently, hardly a semester went by without the university's administration receiving complaints about his demeaning treatment of Christian students. In this professor's classes, academic freedom was supplanted by a requirement to parrot the instructor's leftist views or suffer the consequences. Similar situations exist in many colleges and universities now.

A question we often hear is this: Why do people on the left think they need to revise and rewrite America's history? A veteran we interviewed thought he knew the answer to this question. Bradley commented that so-called progressives on the left have a vision for America that cannot be fulfilled until the vision of the founders is eradicated. An America in which secular humanism is the religion of choice and moral relativism is the guiding principle cannot coexist with an America built on a foundation of Christianity. Nor can it coexist with an America that subscribes to values such as individual freedom, religious liberty, equality of opportunity, personal responsibility, self-reliance, a positive work ethic, fair competition, and the rule of law.

Simply stated, when American history is accurately taught, socialists are shown to be not just ill-informed or misguided but wrong, and they cannot abide being wrong. In fact, they cannot abide even being challenged. This is why Christian and conservative speakers are either banned from college campuses or shouted down on the rare occasions they are invited to speak. It is also why academic freedom, historically the corner-stone of higher education, has been supplanted by politically correct groupthink. Socialists who claim to put great store in the concept of diversity fear nothing more than diversity of thought and opinion.

Evidence of America's Christian Heritage Is Undeniable

Socialists face a real dilemma. They must either rewrite America's history or admit their portrayal of it is inaccurate. This is why they need statues to be taken down, textbooks to omit major portions of the historical record, original documents to remain locked up in dusty archives, and inscriptions etched into granite and stone monuments to be chiseled out. The words of our founders, past presidents, Supreme Court justices, and members of Congress bear witness to our nation's Christian heritage, which is why socialists don't want students at any level to hear their words.

Comments From the Historical Record About America's Christian Heritage

One of the left's favorite founders is Benjamin Franklin, whom they hold up as an exemplar of their secular worldview. But even a cursory review of the historical record belies this contention. Consider these words from Franklin:

> I have lived, sir, a long time, and the longer I live, the more convincing proofs I see of this truth: That God

governs in the affairs of men. And if a sparrow cannot fall to the ground without His notice, is it probable that an empire can rise without his aid? We have been assured in the sacred writings that "except the Lord builds the house, they labor in vain who build it." I firmly believe this; and I also believe without His concurring aid we shall succeed in this political building no better than the builders of Babel.[7]

Thomas Jefferson is also a favorite of revisionists. Socialists use the words of Jefferson, taken out of context, to validate their contention that a wall of separation must be maintained between church and state. But this tactic requires omitting major portions of our third president's writings. Read the following words from Jefferson's pen. Then ask yourself if they are the words of a person who thought the government needed to be protected from Christianity rather than vice versa:

And can the liberties of a nation be thought secure when we have removed their only firm basis, a conviction in the minds of the people that these liberties are the gift of God? That they are not to be violated but with His wrath? Indeed I tremble for my country when I reflect that God is just: that His justice cannot sleep forever.[8]

Jefferson's words are clearly a warning that we ignore at our own peril. The message in Psalm 33:12 is this: "Blessed is the nation whose God is the Lord, the people whom he has chosen as his heritage!" Without directly quoting this verse, Jefferson conveyed its message. His words are a warning against our nation's turning its back on God. This is precisely what many of the veterans we surveyed believe is happening in America.

John Jay, a founder and America's first chief justice of the Supreme Court, left no room for misinterpretation when he said:

> Providence has given to our people the choice of their rulers, and it is the duty, as well as the privilege and interest of our Christian nation, to select and prefer Christians for their rulers.[9]

These kinds of statements made by Franklin, Jefferson, and Jay won't be found in the textbooks used in schools, colleges, and universities today because they convey a message that socialists cannot abide: America was founded on the basis of Christian principles. Students who read these kinds of statements from our founders might be moved to ask some inconvenient questions of progressive teachers and professors.

On March 27, 1854, the Judiciary Committee of the U.S. House of Representatives issued a report that socialists prefer to keep buried. That report reads in part as follows:

> At the time of the adoption of the Constitution and the amendments, the universal sentiment was that Christianity should be encouraged...That was the religion of the founders of the republic and they expected it to remain the religion of their descendants.[10]

Imagine being a progressive teacher or professor and trying to convince students America's heritage is not Christian if textbooks contained these historical statements. If even one minded, critically thinking student happened upon this report from the House Judiciary Committee or any of the other comments from founders in this section, teachers and professors would have a hard time explaining the anti-Christian fiction and progressive propaganda they promulgate.

Eliminating the Evidence of America's Christian Heritage

The evidence presented in the previous section barely scratches the surface of all that is available in the historical record concerning America's Christian heritage. This is why socialists have invested so much time and effort in keeping the record out of the hands of students and everyday Americans. This is why they are doing what James S. Robbins calls "erasing America."

In his landmark book, *Erasing America: Losing Our Future by Destroying Our Past*, Robbins, a senior fellow for national security affairs at the American Foreign Policy Council, documents in great detail the efforts of socialists to tar and feather the Founding Fathers as little more than a bunch of slave-holding racists. It's no longer just Confederate statues being removed; even the names and likenesses of George Washington and Thomas Jefferson are at risk. Some in the progressive community are already lobbying for the destruction of Mount Rushmore, a national monument that includes the likeness of Abraham Lincoln.

Never mind that without George Washington's sacrifices during our War of Independence and later as our first president, there would never have been a United States of America. Washington owned slaves, and in the minds of socialists, that fact alone makes him unworthy of even a mention in the history books, much less the appreciation and respect of a grateful nation. Never mind that Thomas Jefferson authored the Declaration of Independence, served as vice president and president of the United States, and founded the University of Virginia. He owned slaves. Consequently, once again in the minds of socialists, this fact makes him just another bigot unworthy of our attention, much less our honor.

Regardless of what the historical record clearly shows, to suggest America was founded on Christian values is to invite not just criticism but ridicule by progressive revisionists. There is a large and growing element among socialists in America composed of people who are determined to eliminate all evidence of America's Christian heritage. One of the cornerstone issues of those who deny the influence of Christianity on America's founders is the supposed requirement of a wall of separation between church and state.

One of the most pernicious myths ever foisted on the American public concerns the supposed intent of the founders that church and state be forever separated. This myth had its birth in a misguided Supreme Court decision in 1879 (*Reynolds v. United States*) that relied on one paragraph taken out of context from a letter written by Thomas Jefferson. This one paragraph was used to validate that court's misinterpretation of the establishment clause of the First Amendment.

Later, in *Everson v. Board of Education*, Justice Hugo Black used the same out-of-context paragraph from the same letter to justify the court's decision supporting a wall of separation between church and state. Not only did these two cases represent poor legal scholarship on the part of the Supreme Court, but the decisions in both are early examples of an unfortunate practice now common among progressive judges: legislating from the bench.

In the first place, to rely on one paragraph from one letter written by one individual to justify a decision of this magnitude was not just questionable; it was irresponsible. When you consider there are reams of other founding documents on this subject, it is difficult to understand why one paragraph from one letter written by one founder could carry so much weight. Difficult, that is, unless the justices in question made their decisions based on personal bias rather than legal scholarship. The justices in the majority appear to have been looking for a way to validate a decision they had already made, and a sentence from Jefferson's letter, if taken out of context, suited their purpose. This kind of perfidy has become common practice among those who deny the influence of Christianity on the founders and, in turn, on America.

It is true the founders opposed a certain type of divinity, but that divinity was not the God of Holy Scripture. Rather, it was the self-proclaimed divinity of European royalty. America's founders rejected the concept of bloodline superiority. They believed people could be judged superior to one another only on the basis of merit, not birth. This belief is reflected in the Declaration of Independence, which begins: "We hold these truths to be self-evident that all men are created equal; that they are endowed by their Creator with certain unalienable rights..." In other words, the rights of the people, including religious liberty, come not from monarchs but from God. By the way, these words from the Declaration of Independence—"endowed by their Creator"—cause anti-Christian socialists no end of grief. The fact the word "Creator" is capitalized to indicate its reference to God makes them even more uncomfortable.

By the time the founders drafted the Constitution, Europe had a long history of monarchs claiming to be rulers by divine right and then using their power to make their religion the only acceptable and allowable one. The founders rightly rejected the divinity of human monarchs and set about establishing a country in which the people would choose their rulers as well as their religions. Further, the founders expected those who governed as well as those who were governed to be guided by the values and principles set forth in Holy Scripture.

The religion clause of the First Amendment reads as follows: "Congress shall make no law respecting an establishment of religion, or prohibiting the free exercise thereof…" Advocates of a wall of separation emphasize the establishment clause of the First Amendment while conveniently ignoring the free-exercise clause. Over time, this emphasis has transformed the concept of freedom *of* religion into freedom *from* religion, or at least freedom from the Christian religion. This was never the intention of the founders. In fact, they would be appalled.

The founders almost universally encouraged religion and valued its beneficial effects on human thinking and behavior. What they opposed was not religion but state-mandated religion—circumstances in which the only denomination allowed was the one prescribed by those who held the reins of power.

A Veteran Speaks Out

"Progressives believe we are not smart enough to take care of ourselves, so government has to do it. Somewhere along the way, our educational institutions have failed the American people. True history is not being taught, and as a result we have a generation that knows nothing about our Founding Fathers and what they did to create the freedom we enjoy and continue to fight for every day around the world."

—STEVE SABIN, *U.S. Air Force, 1971–2001*

Chief Master Sergeant (retired) Sabin served in the Air Force for thirty years, rising to the rank of senior NCO. His assignments involved supporting a variety of aircraft, including the F-4 Phantom, the KC-135, and reconnaissance aircraft including the SR-71, U-2, and TR-1. For his last assignment, Sergeant Sabin was chosen from among twenty-five Chief Master Sergeants as the senior enlisted advisor to the base commander at Eglin Air Force Base.

A more thorough study of the founding documents would have shown the Supreme Court justices that the brave men and women who risked everything to establish the United States of America had no intention of erecting a wall of separation between church and state. Quite the contrary: The First Amendment was written to ensure freedom of religion, not freedom from it. The establishment clause of the First Amendment—one of the most grossly misinterpreted clauses in the Constitution—was intended to protect citizens from a state-sponsored church that could tax citizens for its support while banning attendance at any other church, the very situation many of the earliest settlers came to America to escape.

It is worth noting at this point, Americans in the late 1700s were overwhelmingly Christian. Approximately 99 percent of them were either Protestant or Catholic. Having made this point, when we state that America rests on a Christian foundation, we are not claiming our country was founded as a theocracy. Rather, we are stating what is obvious from the historical record: Our founders were guided by the moral values of Holy Scripture in their deliberations, beliefs, and subsequent actions. The Christian beliefs of the founders were a powerful force in shaping their views and decisions and, in turn, our nation.

The founders believed people should be free to practice their own religion or to practice no religion without government interference or coercion. They envisioned a nation in which religion was an issue between God and the people, not government and the people. Having said this, it is important to understand peer pressure in favor of the Christian religion was much stronger in the days of the founders, as can be seen in their writings and the state constitutions of the time. In the days of the founders, Christian values were a given, not something debated in the public square or, worse yet, denied by those who chose another course for their lives.

Evidence of America's Christian Heritage

Volumes have been written documenting America's Christian heritage. Consequently, in this chapter, we touch on just a few of the highlights—evidence Christians and unbelievers alike should be familiar with. The evidence of America's Christian heritage abounds. It can be found in the Articles of Confederation, the Declaration of Independence, early state constitutions, the U.S. Constitution, our nation's Capitol and many of our state capitols (carved in stone), and in the words of the individual founders. It can even be found in the historical records of America's first colleges and universities—originally Christian institutions, but they have since become hotbeds of anti-Christian indoctrination.

A Veteran Speaks Out

"The real irony in denying and revising America's history is that not only was America founded on Judeo-Christian principles and values, but all of the major universities originally provided a liberal arts education based on Christian values to prepare students to be productive, contributing members of society. The original focus of American universities was to prepare young men for the ministry and to train other students to be seekers of truth. Today these same institutions blatantly persecute Christian and conservative students while transforming other students into mindless militants through indoctrination and intimidation."

—*SEAN ALAND, U.S. Air Force, 1982–2003*

Lieutenant Colonel (retired) Aland was a copilot and weapons systems officer (WSO) in the F-4E and before retiring also had flights in the F-16, F-18, and AC-130 aircraft. In the immediate aftermath of the September 11 attacks on the Twin Towers and Pentagon, Aland served as director of manpower and personnel (J-1) for the continental U.S. North American Aerospace Defense Command region.

Judging by what is taking place on their campuses today, one would never suspect Harvard, Yale, William & Mary, Princeton, Columbia, Brown, Rutgers, and Dartmouth universities were founded as Christian institutions. The original affiliations of these, America's oldest institutions of higher education, were as follows:

- Harvard: Puritan Congregational
- William & Mary: Anglican
- Yale: Congregational
- Princeton: Presbyterian
- Columbia: Anglican
- Brown: Baptist
- Rutgers: Dutch Reformed
- Dartmouth: Puritan

There is no question America's founders were guided by Christian morals and values in their deliberations, decisions, and subsequent actions. But the roots of America's Christian heritage go back to an event that occurred well before our founding documents were drafted and long before such luminaries as Washington, Adams, Hamilton, Jefferson, and Madison came on the scene.

We take you back in time to September 6, 1620, when a humble but courageous band of pilgrims set out across the Atlantic Ocean aboard a ship called the *Mayflower*. They were undertaking a dangerous trek to America, their purpose being to establish a colony where they would be free to practice their religious beliefs without interference. Packed together on a ship that would be considered tiny by today's standards, this courageous band of believers was willing to risk everything, including their lives, to be free to worship the God of Holy Scripture unimpeded by kings, queens, or government officials.

On the day the *Mayflower* anchored at Plymouth in what is now the state of Massachusetts, the Pilgrim leaders drafted a document that came to be known as the Mayflower Compact. The Mayflower Compact was the first governing document of the Plymouth Colony. That document reads, in part:

> Having undertaken for the glory of God, and advancement of the Christian faith, and honor of our King and Country, a voyage to plant the first colony in the northern parts of Virginia, do by these presents solemnly and mutually, in the presence of God, and one another, covenant and combine our selves together into a civil body politic, for our better ordering and preservation and furtherance of the ends aforesaid; and by virtue hereof to enact, constitute, and frame such just and equal laws, ordinances, acts, constitutions and offices, from time to time, as shall be thought most meet and convenient for the general good of the colony, unto which we promise all due submission and obedience.[11]

This passage reveals that the Pilgrims established a civil government for the purpose of good order, and all of them agreed to submit to that government as long as it was guided by Christian morals and values. The Pilgrims came to the shores of America seeking religious liberty, a fact difficult to deny by even the most ardent historical revisionists. However, historical revisionists solve the problem of the Mayflower Compact by simply leaving it out of most modern textbooks.

In fact, this practice of *selective exclusion* is widely used by socialists bent on imposing their vision of America on students who don't know better. Most of the perpetrators of this unethical practice are highly educated academicians in our nation's colleges and universities who supposedly value intellectual integrity above all else. Textbook publishers ask these subject-matter experts to sit on review committees that make the decisions about what will be included in books in their fields, what will not, and how the included content will be treated. Because many of the decision-makers in textbook publishing are socialists, it should come as no surprise progressive academicians are chosen to serve on their review committees. Using biased review committees amounts to allowing the fox to guard the henhouse, a practice textbook publishers are aware of and complicit in.

A Veteran Speaks Out

"Basic facts concerning historic events do not change. What does change is the way society interprets the facts. It is frustrating when people try to interpret historic events using twenty-first-century standards rather than examining them in the context of the times in which they took place."

—*CHARLES E. "CHUCK" MERKEL JR., Ph.D.*

Dr. Merkel is a graduate of the United States Military Academy at West Point, a professor of history, and a member of the West Point Society with combat deployments to Vietnam and Afghanistan.

Further evidence of the Christian foundation of American government can be found in the proceedings of the first Continental Congress, the founders' first major step toward establishing what eventually became the United States of America. The thirteen colonies took their first step toward unification as a nation when they assembled the Continental Congress in Philadelphia on September 5, 1774. The representatives to the Continental Congress knew what they were undertaking was unprecedented, significant, and of monumental importance. Therefore, they evoked the blessings of God on their proceedings.

In the first action taken by the Continental Congress, its members passed a resolution mandating their proceedings would be opened with prayer. The prayer was duly delivered by a local minister, who also read the thirty-first psalm to those gathered. In this psalm, David states that God is his refuge and strength, his rock and fortress. The psalm concludes with this line: "Be strong and let your hearts take courage, all you who wait for the Lord." Those who advocate the separation of church and state are determined to eliminate not just this kind of religious practice from the public square, but any evidence it ever existed.

After invoking the blessings of God on their work, the delegates to the Continental Congress proceeded to draft the Articles of Confederation, America's first national "constitution." Even a cursory review of the articles shows the delegates were guided by Christian principles in their work. The opening paragraph of the articles includes "...in the Year of our Lord One Thousand Seven Hundred and Seventy-Seven..."[12] Then, in the final paragraph of the articles, the following is included:

And whereas it hath pleased the Great Governor of the World to incline the hearts of the legislatures we respectively represent in Congress…Done at Philadelphia in the state of Pennsylvania the ninth day of July, in the year of our Lord One Thousand Seven Hundred and Seventy-eight…

References to "the year of our Lord" and the "Great Governor of the World" are not the words of unbelievers or people who were religion-neutral, a concept socialists concocted to remove Christianity from public life without seeming to be biased against it. The obvious problem with religious neutrality is there is no such thing. There is no neutrality when it comes to religion. Even those who claim to be religiously neutral have a religion. It is known as secular humanism, and its god is man.

Another way to shed light on the Christian foundation of American government is to study the original state constitutions. Such a study is edifying in that it reveals more broadly the thoughts and beliefs of the men and women who settled this country, not just those who are typically referred to as the founders. Here are excerpts from a few of the original state constitutions, most of which have long since been revised in response to America's drift away from its moral roots and core values:

- *South Carolina Constitution of 1778.* Article 38 of this document states: 1) There is only one eternal God, 2) God should be publicly worshipped, 3) Christianity is the only true religion, 4) the Bible is divinely inspired and should rule both faith and practice, and 5) it is the duty of every man to bear witness to the truth.[13]

- *Maryland Constitution (prior to 1851)*. This document states: 1) It is the duty of people to worship God in whatever way they deem acceptable, 2) Christians are entitled to protection of their religious liberty, and 3) no person should be "molested" because of religion.[14]

- *Delaware Constitution (prior to 1831)*. This document states that no person should be required to attend religious services, but it is the duty of all men to gather together for public worship.[15]

- *Massachusetts Constitution of 1780*. This document required elected officials to take an oath declaring they believed the Christian religion and that it represented the truth.[16] An interesting side note is this clause was written by John Adams, Washington's vice president and the second president of the United States. Ironically, Adams is frequently quoted out of context by anti-Christian detractors who deny America's Christian heritage.

These are just a few examples of the early state constitutions. All of the others contain similar language and expressed similar sentiments until secular humanists gained sufficient political power to recast them in their own politically correct image. It is clear from these early constitutions, the people who settled this country were deeply committed to the Christian faith and were more concerned about protecting religion from government than government from religion.

The people who settled this country did not want the government to be able to compel them to profess a certain religion, or any religion for that matter. Nor did they want the government to be able to tax citizens to support a state-mandated church, as was the practice in European countries. But they did believe the God of Holy Scripture should guide the decisions, actions, and behavior of elected officials as well as the people who elected them.

Another founding document, the Declaration of Independence, clearly supports the fact America's founders were guided by Christian values and beliefs. The first and second paragraphs of the declaration contain the following:

> ...equal station to which the Laws of Nature and of Nature's God entitle them... [A]ll men are created equal, that they are endowed by their Creator with certain unalienable rights...[17]

It is ironic these are the words of Thomas Jefferson, who for years was the favorite Founding Father of those who deny America's Christian heritage. But alas, just as revisionists have finally turned on George Washington, they have also changed their minds about the once venerated Jefferson. In both cases, the bone of contention is slavery. As with all things historical, revisionists judge the lives of people from the past by the standards of today and expect a level of perfection they cannot claim; nor can anyone else. This is hypocrisy at its worst. To condemn the imperfections of historical giants without acknowledging their undeniable contributions to our country is not just a breach of intellectual integrity; it is political correctness run amok.

The U.S. Constitution is not explicitly Christian in its wording, which explains why historical revisionists ignore the other founding documents and hold out the Constitution to validate their anti-Christian biases. But those who use the Constitution in this way aren't reading closely enough. They overlook some obvious Christian references. Per Article I, Section 7 of the U.S. Constitution, presidential vetoes are prohibited on Sundays. This is an obvious display of respect for the one day of the week set aside as the Lord's Day. Further, Article VII states the Constitution was framed "...in the year of our Lord one thousand seven hundred eighty-seven..."[18] These references notwithstanding, one should not expect the Constitution to be filled with explicit Christian references, since it is an instruction manual for self-government, not a philosophical treatise on freedom and the rights of man, like the Declaration of Independence.

Additional evidence of America's Christian heritage can be seen in the words taken directly from the founders. Let's consider the words of just a few of them. John Dickinson, a signer of the Constitution, wrote: "We claim them [our rights] from a higher source—from the King of kings, and Lord of all the earth."[19] John Adams, second president of the United States, made the following statement in 1809: "...there is nothing upon this earth more sublime and affecting than the idea of a great nation all on their knees at once before their God..."[20] Thomas Jefferson, third president of the United States, wrote: "God who gave us life gave us liberty. And can the liberties of a nation be thought secure when we have removed their only firm basis, a conviction in the minds of the people that these liberties are a gift of God?"[21] Like Adams, Jefferson is often quoted—typically out of context—by anti-Christian revisionists to support their contention that America was founded on secular, not Christian, principles. Of course, quotes from Adams and Jefferson such as the ones just cited are conveniently overlooked, omitted, or ignored.

James Monroe, fifth president of the United States, made the following statement in 1818: "When we view the blessings with which our country has been favored, those which we now enjoy, and the means which we possess of handing them down unimpaired to our latest posterity, our attention is drawn to the source from whence they flow. Let us then, unite in offering our most grateful acknowledgments for these blessings to the Divine Author of All Good."[22]

Roger Sherman, who signed the Declaration of Independence and Constitution, wrote: "I believe that there is only one living and true God, existing in three persons, the Father, the Son, and the Holy Ghost, the same in substance equal in power and glory. That the scriptures of the old and new testaments are a revelation from God, and a complete rule to direct us how we may glorify and enjoy him."[23]

Other founders whose views on Christianity are easily accessed and clearly stated include Patrick Henry, John Jay, John Witherspoon, Samuel Adams, George Washington, John Hancock, William Penn, and Alexander Hamilton. It is evident from the words and writings of the founders that in establishing our country they were guided by Christian beliefs, values, and principles. Clearly, Christianity was a powerful force in the lives of the founders, a force that shaped our nation from the outset.

Unfortunately, anti-Christian revisionists have ignored the rules of scholarship and shown themselves to be lacking in intellectual integrity in their ongoing efforts to distort the historical record, particularly as it relates to America's Christian heritage.

Sadly, anti-Christian revisionists control the institutions of education that, in turn, control what America's children and college students are taught. They have used their control to dumb down, distort, rewrite, and reshape American history. As a result, ignorance abounds when it comes to America's Christian heritage as well as America's history in general. There may be no cure for the foolishness of socialists who are so wedded to their anti-Christian, anti-American agenda that facts are just inconveniences to be ignored, but there is a cure for the ignorance they have inflicted on schoolchildren and college students. That cure is called education, as opposed to indoctrination, and all Americans have a role to play in providing it.

Americans who believe in the vision of the founders can play an important role in reversing our nation's drift away from its Christian roots and traditional values. Speak out and inform people who have been indoctrinated rather than educated by sharing the contents of this chapter and challenging them to examine our nation's founding documents as well as the words of the Founding Fathers. But caution them to examine the original documents, letters, and other writings of the founders rather than relying on falsified textbooks and the out-of-context distortions of socialists who are advancing an anti-Christian, anticonservative agenda.

Perhaps the best summary of the views of the founders on the relationship between church and state and on the issue of religious freedom is found in the Vermont Declaration of Rights (1777). Chapter I, Article III of this document reads in part:

> That all men have a natural and unalienable right to worship almighty God, according to the dictates of their own consciences and understanding, regulated by the word of God; and that no man ought, or of right can be compelled to attend any religious worship, or erect, or support any place of worship, or maintain any

minister, contrary to the dictates of his conscience; nor can any man who professes the Protestant religion, be justly deprived or abridged of any civil right, as a citizen, on account of his religious sentiment, or peculiar mode of religious worship; nevertheless, every sector denomination of people ought to observe the Sabbath, or the Lord's day, and keep up, and support, some sort of religious worship, which to them shall seem most agreeable to the revealed will of God.[24]

Before concluding, let's return to the story of the veteran Victoria from earlier in the chapter. After listening to the professor's distorted explanation of the "constitutional requirement" that a wall of separation be maintained between church and state, she raised her hand and asked if she might be allowed to present a different perspective. Not only did the professor refuse Victoria the opportunity, but in words dripping with venom, he verbally attacked her in front of the class.

After class, Victoria was approached by several students who expressed interest in hearing what she had to say. Victoria told them she would write it all down and give them copies at the next class meeting, which she did. She explained the founders' religious views and how those views guided their deliberations and actions. Victoria provided copious documentation to verify her contentions. When a copy of her paper found its way into the hands of her professor, he gave Victoria an F for the class.

Prepared for this likelihood, Victoria filed a formal grievance against the professor with the university's administration. Several students from the class spoke as witnesses on her behalf. One had even filmed the professor's vitriolic outburst on his smart phone. In the end, Victoria passed the course and the professor was cautioned against abusive behavior toward students. In other words, the professor was given a mild pat on the wrist when he should have been fired. This kind of demeaning behavior toward Christians and conservatives is becoming more and more common, not just in college class-rooms but also in the public square.

This chapter is not a comprehensive treatment of America's Christian heritage. Rather, it provides just enough information to demonstrate the need to look deeper into the question with an open mind rather than just parroting the biased distortions taught in educational institutions and reinforced by the main-stream media. Only God can change the minds and hearts of revisionists who are determined to advance an anti-Christian agenda. However, Americans who believe in the vision of the founders might be able to influence the larger audience made up of people who are simply ignorant of the historical record because they were indoctrinated rather than educated.

CHAPTER 4
Secular Humanism, Moral Relativism, and Political Correctness

The premise: "Today there is an overt anti-Christian bias in academia, the media, and the overall culture at large. It is a specific laser-like attack on Christianity and any values that might have even an appearance of having derived from Judeo-Christian scriptures and tradition. The fundamental reason is that the life, death, resurrection, and ascension of Jesus Christ to the right hand of God in human history absolutely obliterates their arguments for the inherent goodness of man and his potential for perfectibility, as well as their grandiose plans for creating an earthly utopia."

—SAM NELSON, U.S. Air Force, 1980–1985

*T*he veteran who expresses the premise for this chapter is Sam Nelson. Nelson is a distinguished graduate of the United States Air Force Academy (1980) with a master's degree from Air University. His civilian career, spanning nearly four decades, has been spent in the research and development of air-launched weapons for the Air Force. During this time, Nelson has helped develop some of the most sophisticated, effective, and lethal non-nuclear weapons in the history of the U.S. military.

Secular Humanism and Moral Relativism: The Religion of the Left

Our featured veteran for this chapter, Nelson, reveals the fundamental flaw of secular humanism: It depends on the perfectibility of human beings. Strive as we might, we humans will never achieve perfection this side of the grave. What took place in the Garden of Eden ensured there would never be a utopia on earth, the claims of socialists notwithstanding. Yet socialists continue to believe they could create a new Eden if they could just gain control of the government and, in turn, the lives of all Americans.

In a speech delivered in 1858 at the Illinois state capitol, then U.S. Senate candidate Abraham Lincoln said a house divided against itself will not stand. In making this statement, Lincoln was paraphrasing Mark 3:25 from the Bible. The house Lincoln spoke of was the United States, and the issue dividing that house was slavery. Unable to reconcile two irreconcilable philosophies, those on the two sides of the slavery issue eventually went to war with each other. Before it was over, America's Civil War would be the bloodiest war in our nation's history. The total number of Americans killed in that devastating conflict is almost equal to the number killed in all other wars the United States has fought.

Fast-forward to today. America is once again a house divided, and the two competing philosophies are as irreconcilable as the antislavery and pro-slavery philosophies in the years leading up to the Civil War. On one side, you have the America envisioned by the founders, an America established on a foundation of Christian principles and built on values such as individual freedom, religious liberty, equality of opportunity, personal responsibility, self-reliance, a positive work ethic, fair competition, and the rule of law.

On the other side, you have socialists who reject America's Christian heritage and core values in favor of government control, secular humanism, moral relativism, and political correctness. These two worldviews are so divergent, one of the veterans interviewed commented she was afraid our country was headed for another civil war. This veteran went on to say the next civil war would be a war of ideas rather than of guns and missiles, but a war nonetheless.

Socialism and its foundational principle of government control have already been explained and, we hope, sufficiently refuted in Chapter 2. Therefore, we will not repeat our arguments against socialism here. Rather, in this chapter we focus on the basic tenets of the religion of socialists who claim they have no religion: secular humanism. We also explain two of the more destructive principles of secular humanism: moral relativism and political correctness. It is important for those who still believe in the America of the founders to understand these concepts and what they mean for the future of our country.

A Veteran Speaks Out

"We serve our country because we love it and what it stands for: freedom of religion, freedom of speech, the pursuit of happiness, and a government for and by the people. If we lose these things, will we still love it? Will we still serve? I would not want my grandchildren to serve if we become a nation that rejects these traditional values."

—GEORGE WILLIAMSON, *U.S. Navy, 1970–1976 and U.S. Air Force, 1982–1995*

Williamson served as an electronics and radar technician in the Navy. In the Air Force, he served as a missile launch officer for intercontinental ballistic missiles (ICBMs) and cruise missiles, and completed his Air Force career as an instructor in the dynamics of international terrorism.

Secular humanism is a philosophy that rejects the God of Holy Scripture. Its followers worship the deity of man. In other words, secular humanists believe man is god. They believe people are fully capable of being ethical and moral without guidance from God or any other source. Secular humanism is the religion of socialists. Its advocates often try to deny that secular humanism is a religion, claiming instead they are religion-neutral. But that argument quickly falls apart on closer examination.

In fact, secular humanism was included as a religion in the Supreme Court case *Torcaso v. Watkins*, in which Justice Hugo Black listed it along with Buddhism and Taoism as religions that do not teach the existence of God. It is important to understand secular humanism is a religion, since socialists are so intent on driving religion out of the lives of everyday Americans. It isn't religion they object to; it's the Christian religion. This explains why secular humanists don't attack other religions such as Islam, Hinduism, and Buddhism, but instead focus all of their negativity on Christianity.

Secular humanism is the philosophical construct undergirding the belief of socialists that man can be perfected on earth, hence they can establish the utopian concept of a workers' paradise. The fact is that there is no such thing as perfection this side of heaven, which explains why the workers' paradise socialists dream about has never been achieved.

There is another glaring problem with secular humanism: When man is god, everyone is god. In other words, there are as many gods as there are people who believe in secular humanism. The problems with this belief are obvious. What happens when one so-called god disagrees with another? Which of them is right? Now multiply this conundrum times millions of people, and what you get is chaos.

Moral relativism is a fundamental tenet of the secular humanist's worldview. It posits that right and wrong are culturally based, man-made concepts; thus, they are subject to determination by the individual. If man decides what is right and wrong, each individual who subscribes to secular humanism can decide what is right or wrong. In layperson's terms, moral relativism means there are no moral absolutes; individuals are empowered to decide for themselves what is right or wrong based on conscience, logic, and reason. An obvious weakness with this belief is sinful people are more likely to decide what is right and wrong on the basis of self-interest than on the basis of conscience, logic, or reason.

One of the veterans from our survey told the story of his grandson's arguing that he, the grandfather, had no right to tell the boy he couldn't skip school and spend the day playing computer games. His grandson had recently been taught in school there are no absolutes when it comes to right and wrong. Each person must decide for himself. The boy decided there was nothing wrong with skipping school and nobody had the right to challenge his decision. Ironically, even the teachers who taught the boy there are no absolute rights or wrongs didn't accept his excuse for skipping school. One wonders if the boy learned anything about the hypocrisy of socialists from this situation. An obvious lesson he should have learned is this: People are free to decide what is right or wrong as long as it comports with the progressive view of right and wrong.

Secular humanists believe in the evolutionary view that life on earth is the result of countless cosmic accidents. To them, life is accidental and random. This being the case, life has no overarching meaning beyond what makes self-absorbed, self-serving, narcissistic people happy in the moment. To secular humanists, anything the individual chooses to do is acceptable because if life is accidental, random, and meaningless, what does it matter in the long run? If there is no God overseeing every aspect of our lives and if there is no heaven or hell, there is no ultimate accountability, so people might as well eat, drink, and be merry.

From the perspective of moral relativists, if something is right for them, it is right, period—a convenient point of view for those who feel constrained by the Judeo-Christian ethic or even secular laws and rules. In adopting moral relativism as part of their worldview, secular humanists are applying a strategy as old as mankind: If the rules get in the way, make new rules. After all, those who make the rules rule.

Is Moral Relativism Really Morally Neutral?

Secular humanists like to claim moral relativism—you do your thing and I'll do mine—is a morally neutral concept. This, of course, is a practical impossibility; nothing is morally neutral. In an article titled "Moral Relativism—Neutral Thinking," the president of Planned Parenthood was quoted as stating that teaching morality should not mean one person imposes his or her views on others. Rather, it should involve sharing one's wisdom, stating one's reasons, and allowing others to make their own judgments.[25]

Sounds good, doesn't it? But there is a problem with her statement a tenth-grade debater could point out. Even a cursory reading of her statement reveals the absurdity of the claim of moral neutrality. The only reason for sharing your wisdom and giving your reasons for believing anything is to influence the thinking of others. If you weren't trying to influence others, you would simply remain silent on the issue in question. Hence, not only is the claim of moral neutrality specious, but arguments in favor of moral relativism are by their very nature self-refuting.

Secular humanists who argue for moral relativism argue against themselves. For example, tell a proponent of moral relativism you advocate child abuse, and you are likely to be reported to government authorities. However, if secular humanists really believe right and wrong are matters of individual choice, how can they argue against child abuse? After all, there are certainly individuals—many of them—who choose to abuse children. This is where the cracks in moral relativism begin to show.

Because of this inherent flaw in their philosophy, secular humanists have taken to adding a disclaimer to their arguments for moral relativism. They say whatever the individual believes to be right is right only if it doesn't harm someone else. But, of course, the disclaimer is as flawed as the concept. When an abortion is performed, the baby is harmed and so is society in general, but secular humanists are among the most vociferous supporters of abortion. Apparently, secular humanists not only get to decide what is right and wrong; they get to decide who is hurt and who isn't by their self-serving decisions, actions, and behaviors.

If it is wrong to harm someone else, why then do college professors who worship at the altar of moral relativism attack Christian students and conservative colleagues? Why do groups such as Antifa (Anti-fascism) sometimes behave like the Fascists they claim to oppose?

Such actions, by their own definition, must be wrong. How do moral relativists justify supporting abortion when the child whose life is taken is certainly harmed, as is the mother, even if she doesn't realize it, not to mention society in general? Moral relativists deny society is harmed by abortion. Oh really? How many future Nobel Prize winners have been aborted? How many people whose research might have cured cancer have been aborted? How many inventors whose innovations might have changed the world have been aborted? How many entrepreneurs who might have created thousands of jobs have been aborted? There is no end to these types of questions, and no acceptable answers to them from proponents of moral relativism.

Human logic is a foundational principle of secular humanism, yet so many secular humanists' actions, arguments, and recommendations lack even a semblance of logic. This is because, unlike Christianity, moral relativism leaves people without an authoritative, unchanging source for determining right and wrong. Moral relativists are like the surveyor who has no definite starting point. Christians, on the other hand, have the never-changing truth of Holy Scripture to rely on when making determinations of right or wrong. Secular humanists have only the fickle, ever-changing whims of human nature.

Obviously, moral relativism is a flawed concept. Nonetheless, it is considered sacred ground among progressive members of academia. For example, a Zogby poll shows 75 percent of college professors teach there is no such thing as right and wrong; good and evil are relative concepts based on individual and cultural interpretation.[26] Yet, these same professors are quick to claim that Christian and conservative worldviews are wrong, or even worse. Robert Brandon, professor of biology and philosophy at Duke University, defended liberal bias at his institution by claiming academicians are smarter than average; conservatives, on the other hand, are not, which explains why his university doesn't hire conservative professors.[27] Brandon's statement underscores why we caution against confusing education with intelligence.

William McGuffey, author of the classic elementary school primers used to teach generations of Americans, claimed that if we eliminate God from our lives, people will be guided by selfishness and sensuality.[28] This was a prophetic statement, because it provides an accurate description of what is happening in America as a result of secular humanism and moral relativism. It is also why so many veterans are concerned about what they see as the declining state of the nation.

Humanist Manifesto: **The Bible for Secular Humanists**

Like most religions, secular humanism has a "bible." Secular humanists look to the *Humanist Manifesto* as their sacred book. There are actually three versions of the manifesto: 1)

Humanist Manifesto I, published in 1933, 2) *Humanist Manifesto II*, published in 1973, and 3) *Humanism and Its Aspirations* (*Humanist Manifesto III*), published in 2003. All three of these books describe a worldview absent God or any other kind of higher power. The God of humanism is the human being. All three versions of the manifesto have been signed by prominent socialists, but not without controversy.

The manifesto has been updated and revised over time, as humanist thinking has evolved and as disagreements among proponents of secular humanism have occurred. As was mentioned earlier in this chapter, when man is god there are bound to be disagreements among all the little gods. The fickle nature of man is just one of many factors that undermine the validity of secular humanism. Consequently, each successive version of the manifesto has sought to correct the perceived weaknesses of the preceding version and reconcile criticisms from secular humanists who disagree on basic issues.

Humanist Manifesto I

The original manifesto was written in 1933. It presented a new belief system to replace religions founded on supernatural revelation. The new belief system it proposed amounted to an egalitarian worldview based on voluntary mutual cooperation among people, an ideal rendered impossible by the sinful nature of man. Predictably, there was disagreement about various aspects of the manifesto among those involved in developing it—a circumstance inherent in all human endeavors. Consequently, the originally proposed title, *The Humanist Manifesto*, had to be changed to *A Humanist Manifesto*.

Ironically, the original manifesto contains a basic tenet that now haunts, embarrasses, and even angers modern-day socialists. It refers to humanism as a religion, something today's socialists go to great lengths to deny, since freedom from religion is the cornerstone of their worldview. If secular humanists were to admit their views of morality are a religion, the hypocrisy of their efforts to remove religion from all aspects of daily life would be exposed. If this happens, socialists would be forced to admit Christianity, not religion, is their real target—something even the most casual observer of American culture would soon realize.

Humanist Manifesto II

The horrors of World War II perpetrated by the followers of Adolf Hitler and Joseph Stalin in Europe and Hideki Tojo in China and the Pacific Islands, exploded the ideal at the heart of the original manifesto. When the evidence of Hitler's death camps, Stalin's pogroms, and Tojo's rape of Nanking was revealed to the world, even the most idealistic of humanists had to admit their hope for a worldwide egalitarian society based on voluntary mutual cooperation might have been a bit optimistic. One can only wonder why the horrors of World War II did not lead humanists to abandon their intellectual and moral relativism altogether. One veteran who responded to our survey commented that if socialists could see some of the things he saw when serving in Vietnam, their beliefs would change overnight.

Admitting the naivety of the first document, drafters of the revised manifesto took a more realistic approach. Rather than pursuing a worldwide egalitarian society based on voluntary mutual cooperation, the drafters of *Humanist Manifesto II* set what they thought were more realistic goals, including the elimination of war and poverty. Of course, they conveniently overlooked the fact if intellectual and moral relativism were valid concepts, there would be nothing wrong with war and no reason to eliminate poverty.

None of the document's authors or supporters thought to ask how these goals could be achieved without changing the hearts of people. Since people are gods, why try to change their hearts? When one will not admit people have a sinful nature, it is easy to naively think war can be eliminated by simply displaying heart-tugging bumper stickers on one's car. After all, displaying slogans such as "Give Peace a Chance" on signs and bumper stickers worked so well in the past, didn't it?

One of the most controversial claims in *Manifesto II* is that people are responsible for what they are and what they will be—gods will not save people; people have to save themselves.[29] Another verse, one that clearly reveals a cherished goal of the left, states the battle for the future of mankind must be fought in the public school classroom by teachers who understand their roles as advocates of a new faith, a religion that recognizes the divinity existent in every human being, a religion that uses the classroom instead of the pulpit to teach humanist values in all subjects and at all levels of education.[30]

As is the case in most human endeavors, there was much disagreement in the progressive community about various aspects of *Manifesto II*. Consequently, only a few ardent proponents agreed to sign the document when it was first released. To solve this problem, the manifesto has since been widely circulated with a caveat making it clear it is not necessary to agree with every detail of the document in order to be a signatory. This disclaimer had the intended effect, and the document eventually garnered more signatures.

Humanist Manifesto III

The latest version of the manifesto—*Humanist Manifesto III*—is titled *Humanism and Its Aspirations.* It was published by the American Humanist Association in 2003. This version of the manifesto is purposefully shorter than the earlier versions. It presents six broad beliefs encompassing the humanist philosophy as professed by the American Humanist Association but leaves plenty of room for interpretation. Leaving plenty of wiggle room in the document was necessary to avoid the kinds of disagreement within humanist circles that undermined the viability of the two previous versions of the manifesto. These six broad statements of belief may be summarized as follows:[31]

- Knowledge of the world is empirically derived (by observation, experimentation, and rational analysis).

- Unguided evolutionary change has the result of making humans integral to nature.

- Ethical values are established by humans and are based on human need that has been tested by experience.

- Humans are fulfilled in life by participating in the service of humane ideals.

- Humans are, by nature, social beings. Therefore, they find meaning in relationships.

- Humans maximize their happiness by working to benefit society.

Although these six statements of belief are not as specific as those contained in the previous versions of the manifesto, they still support the same worldview. For example, the first statement—the humanist belief in empiricism—rules out God's special revelation as set forth in the Bible and reveals an astounding ignorance of the philosophical problems inherent in human empiricism. The second statement is a reiteration of the humanist belief in Darwinian evolution, which of course is a jab at creationism. The second statement is also a justification for supporting abortion.

The third statement makes clear the Bible has no place in establishing right and wrong. Rather, what is right or wrong depends on human need. The last three statements make clear the humanist's rejection of God, the Bible, and religion. In the fourth statement, fulfillment comes from the service of humane ideals, not service to God and His Kingdom. Christians also believe in service, but they know service to people comes from Christ's admonition to love one's neighbor as oneself. In the fifth statement, human relationships are presented as the ultimate goal, as opposed to a relationship with God. Finally, humanists believe service to society is the ultimate service, because for them, man is god. Christians also believe in service to society, but as a way to serve the God who created society and to follow Christ's admonition to love our neighbors as ourselves.

Manifesto III is shorter and more to the point than its predecessors, and its six statements of belief are less specific, but its rejection of God is just as much a cornerstone of the current document as it was in the previous versions. The wording and length of the various versions of the manifesto have changed over time, but its foundational man-as-god philosophy has not. It is this philosophy that causes the unbridgeable gulf between secular humanism and Christianity, as well as the left's intolerance of Christianity.

Secular humanists apparently believe they can peacefully coexist with adherents of some other religions—hence their accommodation of Islam, Hinduism, and Buddhism—but not with Christians. Although there is a philosophical train wreck coming farther down the track involving secular humanists and Islam, for now leftists have focused their animosity on Christianity because they know if Christianity is right, they are wrong. This simple fact concerns secular humanists so much they feel compelled to belittle, attack, and even suppress the Christian worldview wherever and whenever it reveals itself.

Case Against Moral Relativism

To its proponents, one of the appealing aspects of moral relativism is it precludes the need for discussion, debate, and disagreement. There are plenty of people who just want to be left alone to live their lives without the hassle of dealing with issues of right and wrong. These are Americans who live by the motto "I don't want to get involved." They would rather let someone else fight the battles always swirling around them. Moral relativism allows people who shy away from controversy to avoid conflict by simply adopting a "you do your thing and I will do mine" attitude. Of course, the problem with this approach is in doing my thing, I am bound to eventually interfere with your doing your thing.

Perhaps the most appealing aspect of moral relativism to its proponents is it allows them to get away with doing whatever they want. It is the perfect philosophy for people who wish to live their lives unrestrained by rules. This aspect of moral relativism is why national speaker and author Ryan Dobson claims the concept is nothing more than self-centeredness and sinfulness dressed up to disguise its true meaning.[32]

In his book *Be Intolerant: Because Some Things Are Just Stupid*, Dobson states you would never come up with moral relativism by observing the world around you. To claim there are no absolutes in the world is absurd. Consequently, the only way one can believe in moral relativism is to begin with an agenda and then look for ways to rationalize and justify it.[33] This is precisely what progressive advocates of this misguided philosophy do.

Dobson's point is important because one of the foundational tenets of secular humanism is empiricism: Knowledge of the world is gained through observation, experimentation, and rational analysis as opposed to biblical revelation. Ironically, empiricism actually refutes moral relativism. Dobson gives several reasons why moral relativism is a flawed philosophy:[34]

- Moral relativism is empty, meaningless, and purposeless. It can provide permission to do what should not be done or to tolerate what should not be tolerated, but it cannot provide hope. Nor can it give its proponents peace or answers to life's quandaries, problems, or mysteries.

- Moral relativism is self-refuting. To state there are no absolutes—the cornerstone of moral relativism—is to state an absolute.

- People cling to moral relativism in the same way and for the same reason that smokers continue to smoke: they want what it does for them more than they want the benefits of quitting.[35]

Secular humanism is the religion of the left. It has its own bible, *Humanist Manifesto*; its own ethical corollary, moral relativism; and its own god, man. This is not just a clever tactic on our part to render the anti-Christian views of secular human-ists null and void. *Humanist Manifesto* makes clear secular humanism is a religion developed specifically to replace those religions of the world based on supernatural revelation. The facts are clear. Secular humanists do not oppose religion per se, just the Christian religion. There is a name for this point of view: bigotry.

Political Correctness: An Attack on the First Amendment

Secular humanists are masters at inventing polite but misleading names to soften the image of concepts the public might resist if called what they really are. For example, they call abortion "choice" and reverse bigotry "tolerance," but their most misleading term is "political correctness." Few issues raised the hackles of the veterans we surveyed and interviewed more than political correctness.

One veteran called political correctness the antithesis of free speech. Another called it a hoax imposed by the left to prevent the truth from coming out. Another called political correctness blatant thought control. Another called political correctness the biggest fraud foisted on the American public in his lifetime. Yet another veteran said political correctness means you cannot tell the truth if doing so hurts someone's feelings, notwithstanding the fact anyone whose feelings are hurt by the truth is the one with a problem. Not one of the veterans we surveyed or inter-viewed had anything good to say about political correctness. They universally condemned the concept as something insti-tuted by socialists to avoid debates they cannot win on the basis of logic, reason, or facts.

Political correctness may have meant something different when originally conceived than what it has become, but that hardly matters at this point. Political correctness as currently used by socialists is a mind- and speech-control weapon used to prevent challenges to opinions and policies they are unable to defend on their merits. This strategy is as old as human discourse. If you cannot win an argument on the basis of reason, logic, facts, or merit, don't allow arguments in the first place. Instead, stifle disagreement and attack anyone who has the audacity to raise questions. Socialists wield political correctness as a favorite weapon in their ad hominem attacks on Christians and conservatives. Their favorite tactic is to label anything they deem politically incorrect as hate speech.

In commenting on political correctness, the veterans in our survey and interviews expressed the views of many Americans who are tired of being told what to say and how to say it, and then condemned as bigots, racists, misogynists, and hate-mongers when they don't comply. One veteran was emphatic that just making a statement liberals find offensive hardly qualifies as hate speech. Another veteran from our survey made the point the First Amendment was put in place for the very purpose of protecting offensive speech. Inoffensive speech needs no protection. Leftists peddle the fraud of political correctness and constantly engage in name calling because so much of what they profess cannot be defended on the basis of merit. Hence, political correctness represents more than just suppression of conservative and Christian thought; it's an attack on the First Amendment.

Ask socialists what they mean by political correctness, and you will be told it involves avoiding words or statements that might offend other people. Sounds innocent enough, doesn't it? But there are some glaring problems with the concept. We will get to those problems shortly, but first let us clarify terms. Attempting to avoid being offensive or hurtful is called tact, not political correctness. Tact is an outgrowth of good manners. Political correctness has nothing to do with tact or good manners. Rather, it is about controlling what is said, suppressing disagreement, avoiding debate, and muting opposition.

Socialists use political correctness as a bludgeon to avoid being disagreed with, challenged, or called to account. Their favorite tactic is to label people they deem politically incorrect "racists," "bigots," and "misogynists." Smearing people with these kinds of vile pejoratives is a scare tactic to suppress the opinions of anyone who refuses to toe the line of progressive orthodoxy. Socialists use these kinds of labels to frighten those who disagree with them and to prevent them from standing up and speaking out. Take the label "racist," for example.

Because of America's history with race, this term has long held powerfully negative connotations. Hence, just the threat of being called a racist is often enough to scare off those who would otherwise ask questions socialists find inconvenient. But in recent years the term has become so over-used, misused, and abused, it is losing its meaning, not to mention its sting. These days a racist is anyone who doesn't toe the line of progressive orthodoxy regardless of race, life experiences, or actual beliefs.

We have observed white socialists who have never struggled because of their race label black people who fought and suffered in the battles for civil rights as racists. Why? Because these black people had the audacity to be conservatives who worked their way up out of poverty in the same way thousands of other Americans have: without the assistance of a paternal government. The fact these individuals are black, conservative, and successful makes them a threat to the very foundation of the progressive movement.

An obvious problem with political correctness is in these days of hypersensitivity and manufactured outrage, somebody is going to be offended no matter what you say. In a nation of snowflakes and milksops, being offended has replaced baseball as the national pastime. Another problem is political correctness is a one-way street. Christians and conservatives are expected to keep their speech within the boundaries prescribed by thin-skinned socialists, but those same socialists have no compunction about describing Christians, conservatives, and anyone else who disagrees with them in the vilest, most vitriolic terms. Proponents of political correctness are allowed to become offended at the drop of a hat, but Christians and conservatives are supposed to patiently overlook the abuse heaped on them by acerbic, profane socialists.

What makes a term or statement politically correct is determined solely by socialists, who wield the speech-control concept like a sword. Consequently, any statement you make can be ruled politically incorrect if it's not to the liking of socialists. In the same way, any question you ask can be deemed politically incorrect if socialists find it inconvenient or difficult to answer. Political correctness is not a tool to avoid offense. Rather, it's a weapon to stifle free speech.

Here are just a few of the more inane examples of political correctness that have popped up over the years:

- For centuries, the world used the terms "Before Christ" (B.C.) and "anno Domini" (A.D.) in dates. But anti-Christian socialists are offended by any reference to Christ. Therefore, they used political correctness as a club to intimidate people into substituting "Before Common Era" for "B.C." and "Common Era" for "A.D." The stated rationale of socialists for this change is avoiding offense to people who are not Christians. Forget centuries of tradition and the fact Christians might be offended by this politically correct ruse. No matter. Use the historically accurate and traditional terms "B.C."

and "A.D.," and you will be labeled an insensitive religious zealot who cares nothing for the feelings of those who reject Christianity.

- Gender-specific nouns also offend socialists. As a result, committees no longer have "chairmen"; they have "chairpersons." "Manholes" are now "maintenance holes." "Waiters" and "waitresses" are now "waitstaff." The rationale in these cases is to avoid offending women, or so socialists claim. The real rational is the neutering of American society. Use such terms as *actress* or *stewardess* in the presence of a progressive, and you will find yourself labeled a boneheaded, sexist troglodyte.

- Easter eggs are now called "colored eggs" or "festival eggs" to avoid the Christian connection (not that there really is one). According to politically correct socialists, using the term "Easter egg" might offend those who reject the Christian religion. Never mind Christians might be offended by this attack on a longstanding Easter-season tradition. When it comes to political correctness, Christians and conservatives are the only groups not protected.

These examples of political correctness may seem relatively harmless, but they are only the tip of the iceberg. In fact, they are nothing compared with the latest machinations of politically correct socialists. The satire contained in George Orwell's book *Nineteen Eighty-Four* is fast becoming reality. Orwell's only mistake in writing this classic was the predicted date in the title. A central theme in Orwell's classic is mind control through language control. Not surprisingly, this is the goal of political correctness.

If socialists have their way, all Americans will be race-, gender-, and religion-neutral robots lacking any kind of identity or individuality. Rather than being diverse individuals who retain their individuality but come together over a set of commonly held core values, Americans will be neutered automatons programmed to slavishly support the progressive agenda. This fact just underscores how illogical socialists can be. On one hand, they are trying to erase all forms of individual identity, while on the other, they encourage identity politics and tribalism. Students who in the 1960s scoffed at Orwell's satire now realize he was prescient.

The political correctness pièce de résistance in the minds of socialists is their movement to prohibit hospitals from indicating a newborn infant's sex on birth certificates. Further, parents are to be discouraged from choosing gender-specific names for newborn babies. According to socialists, the choice of sex should be left to the child. Yes, you read that right. The more extreme advocates of political correctness believe children who are not allowed to cross the street by themselves should be allowed to choose their own sex.

This move toward gender neutrality is why socialists are trying to eliminate all gender-specific pronouns from the English language. If socialists have their way, politically incorrect pronouns such as "he," "she," "him," and "her" will be replaced by gender-neutral pronouns. To grasp just how absurd the efforts of socialists to neuter American society have become, consider the following list of pronouns socialists have invented to replace their gender-specific counterparts:

- He or she: zie, sie, ey, ve, tey, E
- Him or her: zim, sie, em, ver, ter, em
- His or her: zir, hir, eir, vis, tem, eir
- His or hers: zis, hirs, eirs, vers

To gain an appreciation of just how cumbersome—not to mention insane—these gender-neutral pronouns are, try to use them in a sentence. If socialists have their way, the towels in your bathroom will both be inscribed "eirs" or "vers." The concept of gender-neutral pronouns would be laughable if it were not so serious. By advocating the concept of gender neutrality as a cornerstone of political correctness, socialists are not just denying the natural order of God's world; they are trying to change it. One might reasonably ask what would happen to the propagation of the human race if gender neutrality were to become the norm. But then, as one of the veterans we interviewed stated, propagation is hardly a concern of pro-abortion socialists. Once again, the illogic of socialists is unfathomable.

Political correctness is driving Americans farther apart and contributing to making our nation a house in shambles. Because of political correctness, we have entered the age of identity politics, in which one's race, gender, and sexual orientation are the lens through which the world is viewed. Socialists, in spite of their campaign to achieve gender neutrality, no longer see people as individuals with their own personalities, talents, gifts, assets, ambitions, motivations, and liabilities. How sad. When the heroes of the civil rights movement of the 1960s sang "we shall overcome," it was precisely this kind of thinking they were trying to overcome.

Identity politics is transforming America into a nation of warring tribes instead of letting it be a great melting pot in which people of different cultures, languages, nationalities, and religions find common ground in the vision established by the founders. This tribalism led one of the veterans from our survey to claim America should change its motto from *E pluribus unum* to *E pluribus pluribus*. In a nation as diverse as the United States, tribalism and identity politics are rapidly undoing the bonds which historically united us. Thanks to the unrelenting efforts of socialists, the Balkanization of American society is well underway.

CHAPTER 5

Politics of Destruction and Character Assassination

The premise: "When I see liberals and socialists stoop to name calling, character assassination, and denigration to buttress weak positions they cannot defend with logic, reason, or facts, I am reminded of something we used to say in my Air Force days: 'If you can't dazzle them with your brilliance, baffle them with baloney.' The politics of destruction and character assassination practiced by socialists are just that—baloney."

—HOWARD HILL, U.S. Air Force, 1965–1989
(prisoner of war, 1967–1973)

*T*he veteran who expresses the premise for this chapter is Colonel (retired) Howard Hill, who served in the Air Force and whose father also served in the Air Force. After graduating from the Air Force Academy, Hill was assigned to the 33rd Tactical Fighter Wing in 1966. In May 1967, Hill helped ferry the first F-4D Phantom II jets to Ubon Royal Thai Air Base in Thailand for deployment to Vietnam. In December 1967, Hill's plane was shot down over North Vietnam. He was subsequently captured and became a prisoner of war (POW) for the next five years and two months.

Hill was finally released on March 14, 1973. While he was a POW, his wife, Libby, helped organize and lead the National League of POW/MIA Families. Hill resumed his Air Force career at Andrews Air Force Base. One of his follow-on assignments was service as the principal advisor to the secretary of defense on POW/MIA issues. He later served a tour of duty in the Defense Intelligence Agency (DIA). During his Air Force career, Hill qualified to fly the F-4D, T-39, and C-141, clocking three thousand hours of flight time.

Colonel Hill's military decorations include two Silver Stars, the Distinguished Flying Cross, the Legion of Merit, eight air medals, two Bronze Stars, two Purple Hearts, and the Defense Distinguished Service Medal. He retired from the Air Force in 1989 after twenty-four years of distinguished service to our country. As a civilian, he became a civic leader in his hometown, serving for fourteen years on his local school board and as president of the local PAL soccer league for twenty-five years. In 2019, Hill was inducted into his community's Civic Hall of Fame.

"Politics of Destruction" and "Character Assassination" Defined

Our featured veteran for this chapter, Hill, makes an important point. Name calling, finger pointing, and labeling are tactics socialists use when their positions are weak or indefensible. If their opinions, recommendations, or policies were valid, they would be able to defend them without resorting to bullying tactics. As one of the veterans interviewed for this book said, anytime you have to resort to name calling, you have already lost the argument.

The government envisioned by our founders was one in which elected officials would be chosen by the governed. Those chosen would then serve in advancing the best interests of our nation rather than their own personal interests. These citizen legislators would serve for a period of time and then step aside, honoring the precedent established by George Washington. Our founders never envisioned, nor would they have countenanced, the idea of career politicians whose only aim is to stay in office, amass power, and advance an agenda that undermines the moral foundation and core values of America. But this is precisely what the socialists of today are doing. To accomplish these things, they have begun to engage in the politics of destruction and character assassination.

The politics of destruction is an approach to seeking and retaining elective office that involves demonizing the opposition. Rather than present superior policies or better ideas, those who practice the politics of destruction focus on attacking opponents and trying to destroy them. They apply a principle espoused by Adolf Hitler's propaganda minister, Joseph Goebbels: "If you tell a lie big enough and keep repeating it, people will eventually come to believe it."[36] Before reading further, consider the destruction brought on Germany by Goebbels' principle. America is not immune to destruction from within.

Aided and abetted by the mainstream media, socialists now apply Goebbels' strategy with alacrity. Unfortunately, people are swayed by what they hear on the nightly news, read in their morning newspaper, and download on social media, no matter how biased, ill-informed, and agenda-driven the reports may be. This phenomenon of agenda-driven reporting is what led President Donald Trump to coin the phrase "fake news." Trump is well-placed to know about fake news, since he was the target of it even before he was elected.

The short-term goal of those who practice the politics of destruction is to eliminate any candidates or nominees they don't want elected to office or appointed to the judiciary. The long-term goal is to scare off future candidates by demonstrating what will happen to them should they seek elective office or accept a nomination to a federal court. Clarence Thomas and Brett Kavanaugh are examples of Supreme Court nominees who were viciously attacked by socialists in an effort to undermine their confirmation hearings. Donald Trump is an example of an elected official who has received even worse treatment by socialists. A smear campaign and impeachment effort aimed at him began even before he was elected president.

When the Democrat-controlled House of Representatives voted to impeach Trump in December 2019, that body perpetrated one of the worst political frauds in the history of our nation. This travesty was made exponentially worse by the complicity of some in governmental authority, those specifically tasked to protect and defend against such things. As several of the veterans surveyed and interviewed for this book stated, the Democrats abused the political system in an attempt to remove a duly elected president they could not defeat in a fair election.

The favorite tactic of those who practice the politics of destruction is character assassination. Character assassination involves deliberately seeking to undermine the reputation and credibility of an opponent. Methods favored by those who use this vile tactic include spreading rumors, telling half-truths, manipulating information, defaming, making ad hominem attacks, exaggerating, knowingly making false accusations, and using innuendo and insinuation. How these tactics are used was demonstrated by the attacks of socialists on Clarence Thomas, Brett Kavanaugh, and Donald Trump, to name just three prominent victims.

One of the veterans from our survey commented there were few times in the course of his life when politicians from any party sunk lower than did socialists in these three cases. He commented further that anyone who wants to see what is meant by the politics of destruction and character assassination need look no further than the Thomas and Kavanaugh hearings or the impeachment of Trump. These three examples illustrate clearly what is meant by the politics of destruction.

Consider the example of Supreme Court justice Brett Kavanaugh. He is a highly qualified judge with admirable credentials that make him ideally suited to serve on the Supreme Court. But fearing a conservative majority on the court and, worse yet in their eyes, a vote against *Roe v. Wade*, socialists pulled out all the stops to derail his nomination. They used all the vile tactics associated with character assassination.

The hearings pulled back the curtain to reveal socialists at their worst. Americans had to go all the way back to the Clarence Thomas hearings in 1991 to find a spectacle equal in vitriol and hypocrisy to the Kavanaugh hearings. The venomous attacks on Kavanaugh left an indelible stain on the Democratic Party, but they were just a prelude to what was coming next: the most vile, vicious, and unwarranted attacks in the history of our nation on a sitting president, attacks one of the veterans we interviewed for this book described as an attempted coup masquerading as a political process.

Unwilling to accept defeat at the hands of the American public, socialists in the Democratic Party and corrupt segments of the federal bureaucracy initiated a smear campaign against Trump that began even before his election to the presidency. Their goal was to overturn an election result and regain power without having to risk going to the ballot box, where they might lose again. The coordinated effort between socialists in government and their allies in the mainstream media to destroy Trump and his presidency may be the most shameful example of the politics of destruction in the history of our nation.

Trump was impeached by the Democrat-controlled House of Representatives on a strictly partisan vote. He was then acquitted by the Senate in February 2020. But even his acquittal did not stop the attacks from the left. It appears the politics of destruction and character assassination will continue as long as he is in office and as long as unscrupulous politicians believe these are effective methods for gaining power.

At this writing, the investigation into the possibly trea-sonous acts of some in our law enforcement and intelligence agencies leading to the failed impeachment has not been completed, but we hold out hope the guilty will be prosecuted to the fullest extent of the law.

Several of the veterans from our survey, as well as a lot of other Americans, wonder why there is so much divisiveness and so little cooperation in national politics these days. They want to know why socialists in Congress spend so much time and energy trying to destroy political opponents rather than doing the job they were elected to do. In short, they want to know why elected officials who comprise a government of the people, by the people, and for the people spend so little time and effort actually serving the people.

The answer to these kinds of questions posed by veterans and other Americans is simple but frightening. Cooperation and collaboration are missing from the political process because our country is being pulled away from its moral foundation, core values, and founding vision by socialists who reject the America of the founders. Because of this, we have become the house divided against itself warned of in Mark 3:24—a house that will not stand if things don't change.

Politics of Destruction Erodes America's Moral Foundation

The founders knew republican self-government has one potentially fatal flaw: It works only as long as it rests on a strong moral foundation. Remove the moral foundation supporting a constitutional republic, and you end up with mob rule and elected officials who serve themselves rather than those who elected them. This is the likely long-term result of the politics of destruction. Those who practice this sordid approach to politics not only ignore our country's moral foundation but actually reject it. To them, anything done in the name of feathering their own nests by gaining and retaining power is acceptable. To socialists, the ends justify the means no matter how immoral, unethical, or destructive the means may be.

Without moral restraint, a dog-eat-dog approach to politics is perfectly acceptable—to the bigger dog, that is. The reason progressive ideologues have no compunction against practicing the politics of destruction is they reject the moral foundation and core values upon which our country was founded. They hope to tear down what the founders built and erect a new socialist utopia in its place, an Eden-like nation guided by the principles of secular humanism and moral relativism—a nation they control.

One of the more memorable lines from Abraham Lincoln's Gettysburg Address came when he described the government of the United States as a "government of the people, by the people, and for the people." This hallowed line was stated as a tribute to our republican form of constitutional self-government. However, there is a problem with this tribute Lincoln surely understood but did not mention: A government of the people, by the people, and for the people is, in reality, a government of sinners, by sinners, and for sinners. This is why moral restraints are so important in perpetuating self-government.

The founders understood human nature, which is why they emphasized the need to build our government on a foundation of Christian values. Without this moral foundation, democratic politics always lead to an amoral government in which right and wrong are determined by majority vote. Worse yet, without a strong moral foundation, government serves those who govern rather than the governed. In the process, politics becomes little more than a system for advancing the self-interested agendas of elected officials and government bureaucrats.

When government serves those who govern rather than the governed, the purpose of politics becomes gaining and maintaining power rather than serving the people. This is where we are today, which is why so many Americans have lost confidence in government. The veterans in our survey, along with a lot of other Americans, believe statesmanship and service have been replaced by self-interest and power seeking. This is why, when polled on the subject, citizens rate Congress as one of the least trusted institutions in America, a sentiment echoed by the veterans in our survey and interviews.

Americans are fed up with the partisan bickering, gridlock, exploitation, character assassination, and rank hypocrisy of politics in the twenty-first century. They are tired of dealing with personalities rather than issues. They are tired of socialists trying to destroy opponents rather than offering the American people better policies and better leadership. According to the veterans in our survey, it's time to drag politics out of the gutter and get elected officials focused on serving America instead of themselves.

A Veteran Speaks Out

"Political correctness is behind much of the coverage of violence in America. For example, the media treated the Pulse nightclub shootings as antigay violence, while ignoring the anti-Christian, anti-American motivation of Islamic terrorism perpetrated against the U.S. Further, while mass shootings are horrible, the media completely ignore the fact that they represent only a fraction of the murders committed in dysfunctional cities such as Chicago and Baltimore every year."

—GREGORY HARRIS, *U.S. Air Force, 1982–2011*

Major (retired) Harris served in the Air Force. He was a KC-135 Stratotanker navigator and instructor navigator with almost three thousand hours of flight time. His deployments included service in Japan, Turkey, Germany, and Afghanistan.

Snapshot of Politics in America Today

Supreme Court nominees and political candidates have their lives torn apart by false accusations, innuendo, rumors, and outright lies. Paid thugs, posing as students, incite riots to prevent Christians and/or conservatives from speaking on university campuses. Conservative members of Congress are stalked by protestors yelling profanities, blocking their office entrances, and making threats. Pro-life marchers are attacked by abortion advocates. New York City police officers are openly assaulted by mobs that douse them with water and then throw the empty buckets at them, while onlookers applaud and make videos they post on the internet.

Americans of all stripes, including minorities who have devoted their lives to fighting for civil rights, are labeled "racists," "bigots," and "misogynists" for failing to toe the line of progressive orthodoxy. Campaign rallies devolve into melees with fistfights among supporters of competing candidates. Political debates quickly devolve into shouting matches characterized by childish name calling and finger pointing. Sadly, politics in America has become a gutter sport characterized by excessive partisanship, character assassination, personal animosity, venomous discourse, increasing polarization, smear tactics, tribalism, and even violence.

There are those who claim politics has always been a gutter sport, and the incivility and hostility associated with it in the twenty-first century have always been part of the process. We are quick to admit there have always been bad actors among politicians and the people who elect them. But in years past, the darker side of human nature was always constrained by society's broad adherence to Christian principles. These principles, in turn, encouraged at least a modicum of decorum.

Unfortunately, as America has drifted further and further from its Christian roots, there is less to constrain the sinful nature of people. As a result, the political attacks of socialists are becoming more and more aggressive and vile. Further, these attacks are magnified and multiplied by weaponizing the internet and social media—technologies socialists not only control but use with destructive intent.

According to a study by the Pew Research Center, the partisan divide in America has never been wider.[37] The results of this study show Republicans and Democrats now view each other a) with fear, frustration, and anger; b) as something closer to enemies than opponents; and c) as closed-minded, immoral, lazy, dishonest, and unintelligent. Each believes the policies of the other are bad for our country.[38] The two main political parties are no longer opponents; they are enemies. This is especially sad because enemies can hardly be expected to work together cooperatively for the good of America. Rather, enemies have only one goal: to destroy each other.

Issues Dividing Us

According to a report based on a Gallup poll, the broadening gulf between the views of socialists and the views of conservatives is one of the most significant trends to emerge in U.S. society in the past two decades.[39] The report shows a widening gulf between conservatives and socialists on the following issues:

- Power of the federal government
- Global warming
- Relations with Israel
- Confidence in the police

- Abortion
- Immigration
- Healthcare
- Public education
- Foreign trade
- Trust of mass media
- Gun control
- The environment
- The death penalty
- Taxes
- Relations with Cuba
- Acceptability of having children outside marriage
- Physician-assisted suicide
- Marijuana
- Relations between the races
- Divorce
- Same-sex marriage

The veterans surveyed and interviewed for this book agreed Americans are divided on these issues, but they expressed concern about more than just the specific issues. While there is no question these issues represent major points of contention between the two main political parties in America, the issues are not what most concern veterans. Rather, it is how Americans are engaging one another over these issues. Disagreeing without being disagreeable has become a thing of the past, and because controversy sells, the media encourage disagreement.

As one of the veterans we interviewed commented, when people with differing opinions see one another as enemies rather than opponents, and when they view one another with suspicion, mistrust, and even fear, there is little room for finding common ground or meeting in the middle. When political opponents are viewed as the enemy, the natural inclination is to attack and destroy them. This is the politics of destruction, and it is rapidly becoming the norm in politics in the twenty-first century.

Polarization of Politics: Contributing Causes

When it comes to understanding how politics in America devolved into a gutter sport, there are contributing causes and then there is the root cause. We will save the root cause for last. This section summarizes some of the more frequently stated causes of political polarization, the ones we refer to as contributing causes.

- *Growth of secularism.* The number of professed Christians has declined over the past ten years. At the same time, the Christian church in America—an institution that once influenced the culture—is increasingly influenced by the culture. Because of this, there are fewer constraints on public behavior. One of the inevitable effects of secularization is it encourages and even empowers the darker side of human nature.

- *Rise of tribalism in politics.* Politics used to be about issues, but not any longer. Race, gender, age, sexual orientation, and other forms of group identity have become the most important factors in politics.

One consequence is people approach the political process from the perspective of what divides us rather than what unites us. Americans have begun to view others from a tribal perspective (that is, "If you are a member of my tribe, you are good. If not, you are bad.").

- *Rise of the 1960s generation.* When President John F. Kennedy talked about passing the torch to a new generation, he was talking about the coming of age of what, thanks to Tom Brokaw, eventually became known as the "Greatest Generation." Unfortunately, the children of the "Greatest Generation" rejected the God-and-country values of their parents. In his inaugural address, President Kennedy asked all Americans to focus on the things that unite us rather than the things that divide us.[40] His request was ignored by the 1960s generation, a generation that rejected traditional American and Christian values in favor of drugs, free love, and an "if it feels good, do it" approach to life. Those youngsters of the 1960s didn't birth the progressive movement, but they did drive it further to the left than it had ever been.

- *Death of decorum in Congress.* Historically, members of the U.S. House of Representatives and Senate were expected to adhere to a code of conduct that encouraged courtesy and mutual respect among the members. Over time, the expectations of decorum have fallen by the wayside and been replaced by incivility and ad hominem attacks. In the past, even when they disagreed, senators and representatives were expected to refer to one another using such terms of respect as "my honorable colleague." They are now more likely to use pejorative terms to describe colleagues who disagree with them.

- *Polarization of the media.* There were once standards in journalism, such as expectations of journalistic ethics and objectivity, but those days are gone. Newspapers and television news programs have become partisan advocates for, in most cases, progressive political candidates and organizations. Trial by the media has become a common practice, making character assassination in politics an effective tool for socialists. With some so-called news organizations, political ideology outweighs all other concerns, even including money.

- *Rise of social media.* Even with the blatant partisanship of newspapers and television news programs, there still remain some filters—albeit flimsy ones at best—between what occurs and what is reported, as well as how. This is not the case with social media. On social media, anyone anywhere can say anything about anybody and have it spread across the world in a matter of seconds (unless your message is conservative or Christian, in which case you are likely to be censored by the socialists who control social media). The instant access and relative anonymity of the internet encourage bestial attacks on people whose views differ from those of the writer. They also empower people to make unsubstantiated claims to attack, discredit, or marginalize anyone they want.

These phenomena contribute to the incivility and lack of integrity that currently characterize politics in America. It is important to understand these factors and how they contribute, but it is even more important to understand these factors are not the root cause of the politics of destruction or character assassination. They are contributing causes. The root cause runs much deeper.

Root Cause of Gutter Politics in America

Politics has descended into the gutter in this country because America has drifted away from its Christian roots. All the other supposed causes of this unfortunate circumstance are just secondary to the real cause. The root cause of a problem is the one that must be eliminated if a problem is to be solved. Remove the root cause of a problem and you eliminate the problem. Return America to its Christian roots and you will, at the same time, reintroduce integrity, grace, collaboration, and mutual respect into the political process.

When people fret over the low state of politics in America and wonder what is happening to our country, it is tempting to ask, "Why are you surprised, and what did you expect?" This is precisely what happens when people turn their backs on God. Our founders understood that without a strong moral foundation, their grand experiment in self-government would be susceptible to the worst inclinations of human nature, and they were right. Political discourse in the twenty-first century is indeed being undermined by the worst inclinations of human nature.

America's drift away from its moral roots did not happen overnight. Rather, it has been a slow but steady process that began long ago. The drift can be seen in the declining number of people who profess Christianity when polled. For example, approximately 71 percent of Americans profess to be Christians as of this writing. That sounds like a lot, but it is down from 86 percent as recently as 1990. To put the number of professing Christians into a truer perspective, compare the 71 percent from today with the 99 percent during the days of the founders. Plus, you have to remember these numbers are based on self-identification. Just because people claim to be Christians does not mean they live out their beliefs or are willing to defend the faith against attacks by those who reject it.

When it comes to religion, the fastest growing group in America is comprised of "religious unaffiliated" people. Non-Christian religions such as Buddhism and Islam are also growing.[41] To complicate matters, Americans who profess Christianity no longer hold as strongly to the theological tenets of their denominations as did past generations. In many cases, churches are watering down the teachings of Scripture to become more acceptable to a broader population. Too many churches have forgotten their purpose is to help their members become more intimate with God and thereby morally strong. In other words, the drift away from America's Christian roots is occurring not just in society but in the church too. Society appears to be influencing the church more than the church is influencing society.

Complicity of Academia in Promoting the Politics of Destruction

Colleges and universities in America have played and continue to play a major role in promoting the politics of destruction. No institution in this country has done more to push, pull, and drive America away from its moral roots than academia. This fact is ironic, because in the days of our founders, no institution contributed more to establishing America's moral foundation. But all of this changed almost overnight starting in the 1960s, though the trend was started much sooner. Since that time, by serving as incubators for and proponents of secular humanist thought, colleges and universities have used their substantial influence to promote the politics of destruction.

Colleges and universities preach tolerance while practicing the opposite. They indoctrinate and manipulate morally and intellectually malleable students, transforming them into ardent acolytes of the progressive agenda. One of the veterans in our survey commented that going away to college so transformed her favorite nephew she didn't even recognize the young man anymore. While at college, her nephew became a completely different person, and in the worst possible ways.

The young man was indoctrinated by progressive professors to the point of becoming an ardent leftist and advocate of the politics of destruction. Worse yet, he did this while pursuing an unmarketable college major and accumulating a mountain of student debt he now expects the American people to pay. By substituting indoctrination for education, colleges and universities have ensured students are immersed in the progressive point of view on all issues and no other view gets a fair and impartial hearing. In many cases, nonprogressive views get no hearing at all.

The changes that have occurred in higher education since the days of our founders are truly disturbing. As mentioned previously, the earliest colleges and universities in America were all church-affiliated institutions. Harvard University, located in Cambridge, Massachusetts, is considered by many to be the flagship university in this country. Founded in 1636, the university is named after an early benefactor, John Harvard, a minister who bequeathed his library and half of his estate to the institution. Harvard's original mission—one far from its current mission—was to train ministers. John Winthrop was the first governor of the Massachusetts Bay Colony. Consider his description of Harvard's founding:

> After God had carried us safe to New England, and we had built our houses, provided necessaries for our livelihood, reared convenient places for God's worship, and led the civil government, one of the next things we longed for and looked after was to advance learning and perpetuate it to posterity...And as we were thinking and consulting how to effect this great work, it pleased God to stir up the heart of one Mr. Harvard (a Godly gentleman and a lover of learning, there living among us) to give the one-half of his estate...toward the founding of a college...Over the college is Master Dunster...who has so trained up his pupils in the tongues and arts, and so seasoned them with the principles of divinity and Christianity, that we have to our great comfort (and in truth) beyond our hopes, beheld their progress in learning and godliness also.[42]

Most of Harvard's early graduates became ministers. For years the college's motto was *Veritas Christo et Ecclesiae*, which is Latin for "Truth in Christ and the Church." This motto has since been shortened to just one word: "*Veritas*," meaning truth. Unfortunately, Harvard no longer accepts Christ or the Bible as the source of truth, a fact rendering this motto meaningless.

An early president of the institution, Increase Mather, eventually grew disenchanted with what he saw as the liberal views of Harvard's faculty and resigned as president. He and his son, Cotton Mather—a Puritan minister, historian, and prolific writer—helped establish a new college: the Collegiate School of Connecticut, now known as Yale University. The other founders of Yale were Congregationalist ministers. The university's current name came from a businessman from Wales, Elihu Yale, who donated the money to build a new facility for the school. A Yale graduate is known as an "Eli" in honor of Elihu Yale. Yale and its longtime rival Harvard have transformed themselves over the years from Christian institutions into bastions of anti-Christian bias.

The same movement away from Christianity has occurred at all of America's earliest institutions of higher education. Princeton University, in Princeton, New Jersey, was founded in 1746 by four ministers. Its original board of trustees was composed of Presbyterians, Quakers, Episcopalians, and a member of the Dutch Reformed Church. Columbia University, in New York City, was founded in 1754 as King's College with a charter from King George II of England. Its roots, therefore, are in the Anglican Church. Brown University, in Providence, Rhode Island, was founded in 1764 and had Baptist and Congregationalist ties. Its original motto was *In Deo speramus*, which is Latin for "In God we hope." Rutgers University was founded in 1766 by ministers of the Dutch Reformed Church. Dartmouth College, located in Hanover, New Hampshire, was founded in 1769 by a Puritan minister, Eleazar Wheelock.

All of these well-known universities were founded by Christians on the basis of Christian principles. Unfortunately, over time they have strayed far from their roots. In fact, it would be hard to find organizations less friendly to Christianity in America today. Some institutions of higher education in this country are downright hostile to Christianity. There was a time when institutions of higher education in this country could be relied on to inculcate traditional American values—including Christian values—in students. Now it is more common for colleges and universities to oppose these values and denigrate, demean, and abase anyone who subscribes to them.

A Veteran Speaks Out

"Liberals and members of the semisocialist Democratic Party are in dire need of learning how to disagree without being disagreeable and combative. The left's ongoing war against conservatives and conservative ideology represents the new normal for them. Today's liberals would rather attack conservatives with toxic labels ("racist," "homophobe," "fascist," etc.) than actually debate ideas on their merits. One reason liberals so readily resort to character assassination is that doing so is easier than debating the logic and facts, and for the most part no one calls them on it—certainly not the mainstream media."

—*Skip Hull, U.S. Marine Corps, 1975–1978*

Hull served as battalion supply officer for the 3rd Battalion, 4th Marines and ordnance officer for headquarters and service battalion, 2nd Marine Division.

Other Signs of America's Drift Away From Its Moral Roots

One of the benefits of getting along in years is you gain a perspective that comes only with age. Although there are several excellent studies available which document things such as the decline in church attendance, the number of churches closing down every year, and the percentage of young people who leave the church, you don't need to rely on dry statistics for evidence of America's drift away from its moral roots. Just look around you.

One of the veterans interviewed for this book spoke of how different things were when he was a youngster. When he was in public elementary school, each school day began with reciting the Lord's Prayer, listening as the teacher read a passage from the Bible, and reciting the Pledge of Allegiance. When students got in trouble, the teacher made them copy pages out of the Bible or memorize a Bible verse and recite it in front of the class. Try to imagine these things happening in a public school classroom today. In high school, this veteran played football. Before every game, a local pastor prayed for both teams, a practice that has become so controversial most public schools have dropped it.

Perhaps the most striking evidence of America's drift from its moral roots can be seen in the *normal* behavior of everyday Americans. Think of all the behaviors you observe routinely that violate the second half of the "greatest commandment," in which Christ told us to love our neighbors as ourselves: rudeness, incivility, road rage, mass shootings, workplace violence, vulgar music lyrics, character assassination in politics, attacks on police officers, rampant profanity, epidemic cheating, internet "flaming," cyberbullying, sideline rage, gratuitous sex and violence in the movies, on television, and in computer games, and lest we forget, abortion on demand.

Let's take a closer look at one of the more frequently used character assassination tactics of socialists to suppress opposition to their views: calling people "racists." In his syndicated column of July 31, 2019, Walter Williams—professor of economics at George Mason University—made an important point. His column was titled "Being a racist is easy today."[43] Williams, who is a black American old enough to remember real racism, chronicles some of the hateful actions of people who were racists back when the term actually meant something. He recalls the burning crosses of the Ku Klux Klan; Lester Maddox, onetime governor of Georgia, using an ax handle to keep black Americans out of white-only restaurants; and Bull Connor, onetime police commissioner in Birmingham, Alabama, turning fire hoses and snarling police dogs on civil rights demonstrators.[44]

Williams states clearly in his column that when progressives/socialists cannot win an argument, they falsely label their opponents "racists," which is why the term has lost its meaning and much of its sting. He goes on to write how black Americans his age should explain what real racism is, not to correct the false labeling of white socialists but to accurately inform young black people.[45] Just disagreeing with a liberal or besting one in an argument does not make someone a racist. Young people of all races need to understand that.

Try to square the kinds of destructive, hateful behaviors that have become so common in American society with the teachings of Scripture. Ephesians 4:32 admonishes us to be kind and compassionate to one another and to forgive one another just as Christ forgave us. Verse 1 Peter 3:8 admonishes us to love one another and to be compassionate and humble. Colossians

3:12 tells us to wrap ourselves in compassion, "kindness, humility, meekness, and patience." People who internalize these lessons from Scripture do not engage in the politics of destruction, character assassination, or the other behaviors coarsening American culture.

The further our country strays from its moral roots and core values, the more often we encounter the dark side of human nature in our daily lives. It is the worst inclinations of human nature being acted out by socialists who practice the politics of destruction and character assassination, practices that are threatening the future of the great experiment in constitutional republican self-government undertaken by our founders all those years ago. If the great experiment fails, all Americans —left, right, and center as well as believers and unbelievers— will suffer.

CHAPTER 6

Porous Borders and Sanctuary Cities

The premise: "*Today the protections we have under the Constitution are subverted by leftist tyrants who use the power of the state to exploit those who biblically deserve to have the rule of law under our Constitution—a law which is in harmony with God's definition of freedom as well as right and wrong. Ironically, they use the attractions of America's success to entrap illegal aliens and protect them by destroying the rule of law, Constitutional protections, and the freedoms of the Citizens they are elected to protect.*"

—ROBERT L. "BOB" GRETE, Ph.D., U.S. Air Force, 1958–1980

The veteran who expresses the premise for this chapter is Dr. Robert L. "Bob" Grete. Dr. Grete began his career in the military at the United States Military Academy at West Point, where he earned a bachelor of science degree in 1958. He retired from the Air Force in 1980 after twenty-one and a half years of distinguished service to his country. An Air Force pilot, Dr. Grete had more than 5,700 flying hours when he retired.

Foreign duty during his career included tours in Vietnam, Thailand, Germany, and Korea.

In Vietnam, Dr. Grete served as an airborne forward air controller (FAC) flying the O-2A aircraft. In recognition of his distinguished and courageous service in Vietnam, he was awarded the Distinguished Flying Cross, two Silver Stars, three Meritorious Service Medals, thirteen Air Medals, an Army Commendation Medal, and numerous other decorations. From 1963 to 1967, Dr. Grete served as an instructor and assistant professor in the Department of Social Sciences at the United States Military Academy at West Point, where he taught economics and the economics of national security.

Why Socialists Want Open Borders

Our featured veteran for this chapter, Dr. Grete, makes an important point about liberal politicians who advocate for open borders. These members of Congress were elected to serve and protect American citizens, not immigrants who enter our country illegally and are breaking the law every day they remain here. Perhaps these progressive members of Congress should be reminded by voters where their loyalties are supposed to lie.

Do you have locks on the doors of your home? Do you have a fence around your yard? A lot of Americans do. We lock our doors and fence our yards to prevent people from entering our homes illegally. We do these things to protect ourselves and our families. Not only is securing your home a fundamental right; it is the smart thing to do. In these days of home invasions and drug-related break-ins, leaving your home open to illegal entry is not just unwise; it is irresponsible. The same can be said for our country.

Home security is a growth industry in our country. Since socialists are just as likely as anyone else to have locked doors, fenced yards, and security systems, why do so many of them oppose the same kinds of security at America's borders? A nation that cannot secure its own borders is not a sovereign nation. America is just like you vis-à-vis your home. Our country has a right and an obligation to prevent people from entering illegally. Protecting our nation's citizens is the most important responsibility an American president has.

There is no universal agreement within the Democratic Party concerning border security. In fact, the party is fractured over the issue. Some Democrats oppose border security simply because they associate the issue with Donald Trump. Other Democrats want to stick their heads in the sand and avoid immigration altogether, viewing it as a no-win issue. Some Democrats even claim to believe Americans don't want border security. These Democrats believe those who demand border security are out of touch with their fellow Americans on the issue. Polls on the subject suggest otherwise.

In a Gallup poll on the issue, 47 percent of respondents indicated they view illegal immigration as a serious threat to America's interests. Worse yet for Democrats, a poll conducted by Quinnipiac University reveals that 60 percent of respondents think Democrats are more interested in exploiting immigration for political gain than solving the problem. Democrats have been quick to attack proposals to ensure border security, but they steadfastly refuse to offer alternative solutions. In fact, the only solutions Democrats have proposed are open borders and the elimination of Immigration and Customs Enforcement (ICE).

A Veteran Speaks Out

"The inscription on the Statue of Liberty that reads 'Give me your tired, your poor, your huddled masses yearning to breathe free...' was not intended as an open invitation for immigrants to come to America illegally and then expect our citizens to conform to the failed ideas and ideologies of the countries they left behind."

—MARK NORRIS, *U.S. Air Force, 1981–2004*

Master Sergeant (retired) Norris was awarded the Airman's Medal for heroism involving voluntary risk of life near Ahmed Al Jaber Air Base, Kuwait, in December 1999, when he took charge during a crash landing of a C-130 aircraft and rescued injured passengers in the aftermath of the crash.

Although the Democratic Party as a whole has waffled on the issue of immigration and done its best to avoid it, far-left socialists within the Democratic Party have broken ranks and made their views known. Because this element of the Democratic Party is making the most noise on the issue, it is getting the most media attention. Socialists are clear concerning what they want when it comes to immigration policies: open borders and the elimination of ICE. But to the majority of Americans, open borders are a frightening prospect. Americans rightfully fear opening the country to drug cartels, disease, gang activity, and hundreds of thousands of new immigrants who would become a drain on the federal treasury. These are legitimate concerns.

Why then do the more liberal progressives in the Democratic Party want open borders? To answer this question, let us return to our summary of the progressive agenda from Chapter 2. We explained that agenda as follows:

Step 1: The government controls the people.

Step 2: Socialists control the government.

Step 3: Socialists control the people.

Having open borders is a strategy of socialists for achieving Step 2 of their agenda and, ultimately, Step 3. They understand the immigrants flooding our southern border are coming from some of the poorest countries in the world including Honduras, Guatemala, and El Salvador. They also know these immigrants are coming to the United States in the hope that our government will take care of them, something the governments of their home countries could not do.

The opportunities many of these immigrants from the poorest countries seek are free healthcare, free education, free childcare, and welfare. This view of American opportunity makes immigrants from poverty-stricken countries dependably malleable subjects of big-government progressives and socialists. As one of the veterans we interviewed for this book commented, socialists know they can count on the support of people who feed at the public trough. Consequently, they want to increase the number of those people.

Socialists who are willing to do anything to gain and maintain power, no matter the consequences, view opening the border as just another short-term strategy for gaining control of the government and, in turn, the governed. Their unstated but unalterable goal is to control you and me. They are perfectly content to ignore the long-term consequences of open borders.

In fact, as those long-term consequences begin to be felt, socialists will do what they always do: sidestep the issue and point the finger of blame at those who tried to warn them.

Why It's Important to Secure America's Borders

Thousands of individuals enter America illegally every year, a fact socialists find acceptable. But we ignore illegal immigration at our own peril. There are good reasons it is important to secure America's borders. Those reasons are related to:

- National sovereignty
- Safety/security
- Health
- American jobs
- Cost
- Taxes

Democrats in Congress have stubbornly refused to take action to secure the borders, but President Trump has refused to let the issue of border security fall between the cracks. In standing firm on border security, Trump—though vilified by socialists—has been guilty of nothing more than carrying out two of his most important responsibilities as president: 1) protecting America's national sovereignty and 2) ensuring the safety and security of American citizens. A nation that cannot or does not control its own borders is no longer a sovereign nation. Sovereignty is the authority of a nation to govern itself. America is not governing itself when other nations are allowed to determine who becomes a resident of the United States. When other countries are allowed to export their citizens, including criminals, to the United States, our country has ceded its sovereignty to them. Failing to secure and control our own borders threatens the safety and security of American citizens. Illegal immigration increases the threats posed by the illegal drug trade, human trafficking, criminal gangs, and illegal weapons as well as by terrorists who might enter America through our unsecured border. Of the approximately sixty thousand criminal cases brought by federal prosecutors in a given year, more than 40 percent occur in court districts near the southern border.[46]

Porous borders also increase the likelihood of infectious diseases being brought into the United States. When the Zika virus and swine flu outbreak occurred several years ago, they were spread at least in part by illegal immigrants.[47] When people enter the country illegally, it is difficult if not impossible to control the diseases they bring with them.

With legal immigration, infectious diseases can be detected, monitored, treated, and, as a result, controlled. As of this writing, the bubonic plague has become a real threat in American cities with high rates of homelessness, such as the sanctuary cities of San Francisco and Los Angeles. Rats attracted by the human waste and garbage found in the tent cities of the homeless—prime locations for illegal immigrants who come to the U.S. with no place to stay—carry and spread diseases long thought to be wiped out.

Then there are the previously unidentified new strains of disease like COVID-19, discovered in 2019. Do we really want to go through another pandemic after the COVID-19 one? Without border sovereignty, the next virus strain could have us enduring much, much bigger problems than a toilet paper shortage. With porous borders, our nation could collapse under the weight of tens of millions of people going to hospitals and many to their graves.

Protecting American jobs is another reason for enforcing border security. Every job taken by an illegal immigrant is one that could have been filled by an American citizen. Democrats in Congress are quick to attack this contention, claiming immigrants have the same right to a job as any American citizen. The fallacy of their argument is members of the United States Congress are elected to serve American citizens, not illegal immigrants.

Expecting Americans to pick up the tab for the increased costs of government services caused by illegal immigration does not sit well with the veterans we interviewed and surveyed for this book. Nor does it sit well with a lot of other Americans. At this writing, it is estimated the cost of providing amnesty to the ten million illegal adult immigrants in the United States would exceed $1.2 trillion, which is more than $15,000 per taxpaying household.[48] Imagine receiving a letter from the Internal Revenue Service (IRS) claiming you owe an additional $15,000 over what you have already paid in a given year to cover the costs of supporting immigrants illegally in the U.S.

How America Can Secure Its Borders

Donald Trump ran for president on a platform that included building a wall across America's southern border. A lot of Americans must have agreed with his idea. After all, in spite of media predictions to the contrary, Trump won the election against Hillary Clinton, who opposed the wall. The idea of a wall makes sense to Americans because they do the same thing to prevent illegal entry into their property. They put up fences. The wall is a good idea, but by itself it won't be enough. In addition to the wall, a number of other security measures will have to be implemented or improved if America's southern border is to be secured:[49]

- *Streamline the deportation process.* As things stand now, liberal attorneys are allowed to intervene in the processing of illegal immigrants in ways purposefully created to cause a backlog. Whether or not to deport people who enter this country should be a simple binary decision. Are they here illegally? If the answer is yes, they should be deported immediately. If the answer is no, the processing of their application to stay should begin immediately. Attorneys should not be allowed to gum up the process by creating supposed legal gray areas.

- *Illegal immigrants should be detained until they have had their deportation hearings.* Allowing illegal immigrants to use public services and even work while waiting for a hearing on their cases is bad policy. It is not uncommon for unscrupulous employers to hire illegal immigrants who are waiting for their deportation hearings and even give them safe haven, thereby thwarting the legal immigration process. Illegal immigrants should be detained, and the detention time should be short (see the first recommendation above).

- *Fix DACA.* Deferred Action for Childhood Arrivals (DACA) is an immigration policy implemented during the Obama administration to deal with the issue of illegal immigrants currently in the United States who are under the age of thirty-one (as of June 15, 2012) and who have been here

continuously since June 15, 2007. As is often the
case with federal legislation, DACA has led to
more questions than answers. President Trump has
proposed improvements to DACA, but Democrats
in Congress have ignored his recommendations.
Passing legislation based on Trump's recommendations would clean up the confusion and answer
many of the questions that have rendered DACA
ineffective. His recommendations are to: 1) put a
cap on chain immigration, 2) end the visa lottery
program, 3) mandate employment e-verification,
and 4) fine employers who circumvent the law and
hire illegal immigrants. Democrats in Congress
have refused to act on any of these recommendations, and instead have condemned them without
offering any realistic alternatives.

▪ *Use the National Guard, military, and intelligence
services as appropriate in controlling entry into the
United States.* Although there are limits to the
roles the National Guard, military, and intelligence services can play in securing the borders, the
services they can provide could be vital. The use of
these three in helping secure America's borders is
covered in the next section.

When considering the issue of immigration in the broadest
sense, it is good to decide at the outset where your loyalties lie. Socialists abhor the phrase "America first," but they
are completely out of step with American citizens on this
issue. Socialists may not like the idea of putting America first,
but Americans do. As one of the veterans from our survey

commented, politicians who don't put America first should be turned out of office. If they want to put the interests of people from other countries ahead of those of American citizens, they should run for office in those countries.

Using the National Guard and Military for Border Security

Responsibility for securing America's borders rests with the Department of Homeland Security (DHS). The component within DHS with primary responsibility for border security is U.S. Customs and Border Protection (CBP). Within CBP, the U.S. Border Patrol is tasked with detecting and preventing illegal immigration into the United States. The missions of the military service branches, including the Army National Guard and Air National Guard, do not specifically include border security. However, both the military and the National Guard can be called on to support CBP and the Border Patrol in carrying out their missions.

The National Guard is a reserve force with the mission of maintaining units equipped, trained, and ready on short notice to mobilize for war or other national emergencies. There is also an Air National Guard. Authority for the National Guard and Air National Guard is shared by the governors of their respective states and the president of the United States in his capacity as commander in chief.

When operating under the authority of the president, these reserve units are referred to as the National Guard of the United States and the Air National Guard of the United States. When operating under the authority of governors, these units are typically referred to as the National Guard and Air National Guard.

Organizationally, the National Guard is attached to the U.S. Army and the Air National Guard is attached to the U.S. Air Force, but they should not be confused with the Army Reserve or the Air Force Reserve.

The National Guard has been mobilized to maintain order and assist victims in the aftermath of natural disasters, prevent violence and looting in the midst of civil unrest, interdict illegal drugs, and, more recently, to help immigration authorities secure America's southern border. In these cases, the authority for expanding the mission of the National Guard comes from Section 502(f) of Title 32 of U.S. Code. Title 32 allows National Guard troops to be used in capacities other than those normally prescribed, provided they are given federal pay and benefits during the duration of their expanded duties. In 2018, pursuant to Title 32, the Trump administration authorized the deployment of up to four thousand Army National Guard troops to America's southern border.

The military service branches—Army, Navy, Air Force, and Marines—are less likely than the National Guard to be used for border security. This is because they are restricted by the Posse Comitatus Act (PCA) from performing civilian law enforcement duties except when given specific authority to do so. Activities prohibited by Department of Defense (DOD) Directive 5525.5 include: 1) interdiction of ground, air, or seagoing transport, 2) search and seizure, 3) arrest and apprehension of suspects, and 4) serving as undercover agents, informants, interrogators, or investigators. All these activities are considered direct law enforcement responsibilities. Two exceptions to the prohibitions in DOD Directive 5525.5 are in the cases of responding to sudden emergencies and protecting federal property.

On the surface, it might appear DOD Directive 5525.5 rules out involving the military in any kind of border-security role. However, in Chapter 18, Title 10, U.S. Code, Congress authorizes the military to provide specifically enumerated types of assistance to law enforcement authorities when the need arises. This assistance includes sharing information, loaning equipment and facilities, providing training and expert advice, and maintaining and operating equipment. The military services are limited in what they can do to help secure America's borders, but they can play an important role should the need arise.

Using America's Intelligence Assets for Border Security

Most of the activities of America's intelligence community are classified. Consequently, specifics concerning any role they might be playing in border security are not available. However, even though border security is not specifically part of the missions of federal intelligence agencies, protecting the United States from foreign threats is. Matters with a bearing on homeland security, such as monitoring the activities of international terrorist groups, are part of the intelligence community's mission. Since one of the reasons border security is so important is that terrorists posing as immigrants might gain entry to the United States, the intelligence community has at least an indirect role to play.

The federal intelligence community collects and analyzes data relating to homeland security and terrorist threats. This information can be shared as appropriate with law enforcement and immigration authorities. Possible uses of the intelligence community's assets to assist with border security include the following: 1) satellite reconnaissance, 2) electronic surveillance, 3) human intelligence, and 4) analysis of open-source material in the media of other countries. These kinds of assets are not likely to be focused solely on border security, nor should they be. However, helpful information they uncover can and should be shared with appropriate law enforcement and immigration authorities.

Sanctuary Cities

When it comes to the issues causing concern, frustration, and even exasperation among the veterans in our survey, sanctuary cities rank high on the list. A sanctuary city is a specific municipal jurisdiction that either refuses to cooperate with federal authorities on immigration matters or severely restricts its cooperation. The arguments made by socialists in support of sanctuary cities are generally the same arguments they make for open borders, but with one addition. Socialists like to say since there are no physical borders between cities or states within the United States, people living in sanctuary cities who disagree with the concept are free to move to any other city or state of their choice.

This, of course, is a specious argument. People have homes, lives, jobs, friends, family, churches, and other important ties that make it difficult, if not impossible, to simply pick up and move to another city or state if they don't like living in a sanctuary city. This is a growing problem for a lot of Americans because, including cities, counties, and states, there are now more than five hundred sanctuaries for illegal immigrants in the United States. Sanctuary cities do a number of bad things to America, as follows.

Sanctuary Cities Encourage Illegal Immigration

People who decide to come to America illegally know before they arrive at our border which cities, counties, and states will offer them sanctuary. Knowing sanctuaries exist, why would anyone submit to the legal immigration process? Consequently, sanctuary cities, counties, and states encourage illegal immigration. They are magnets for illegal immigrants.

A Veteran Speaks Out

"Sanctuary cities are an affront to the rule of law. No individuals I am aware of would leave their doors unlocked and expose their loved ones to danger. The thinking behind sanctuary cities is inexplicable and speaks to a worldview far from the one that made America great."

—ANDREW M. BENO, *U.S. Air Force, 1983–2003*

Major (retired) Beno served as a senior navigator with more than 4,200 flying hours in Special Operations MC-130 Combat Shadow aircraft. He served in combat in Panama, Iraq, and Afghanistan.

Sanctuary Cities Protect Criminals From Deportation

Socialists like to claim illegal immigrants are less likely to commit crimes than American citizens. This may or may not be true. Of course, it is possible, since illegal immigrants try to fly below the radar to keep from being discovered by law enforcement authorities until they can reach a sanctuary city. Illegal immigrants who fly below the radar are like the drunk driver who loses his license but continues to drive. He never exceeds the speed limit, for fear of being caught and having his status as an illegal driver revealed. But socialists who claim most illegal immigrants obey the law are missing an important point.

As one of the veterans from our survey commented, illegal immigrants are breaking the law by just being here, and are breaking it again every day they stay. Further, statistics on crimes committed by illegal immigrants are unreliable for a variety of reasons, the most prominent of which is there is no comprehensive database maintained on this subject. Regardless of the number of crimes illegal immigrants commit compared with American citizens, those who do commit crimes should be deported, permanently.

Two high-profile cases involving illegal immigrants who committed crimes make the point. The Mollie Tibbetts murder by an illegal immigrant in 2019 speaks louder than unreliable statistics ever could. Tibbetts, a University of Iowa student who disappeared on July 18, 2018, was killed by an illegal immigrant who was working near the university under a false name. Her parents are not likely to be comforted by progressive claims that illegal immigrants are generally law-abiding.

Another high-profile case involving an illegal immigrant is the fatal shooting of Kathryn Steinle in July 2015. Steinle was shot as she strolled along Pier 14 in San Francisco with her father and a friend. A California jury acquitted the illegal immigrant who shot Steinle, accepting his claim that the gun fired accidently. But serious questions remain. First, what was an illegal immigrant doing with a gun in the first place? Second, what was the perpetrator doing in the United States, since he had been deported five previous times and was on probation in Texas? Since San Francisco is a sanctuary city, there is little question as to why the man who shot Steinle was there.

The cases of Tibbetts and Steinle are just two representative examples of numerous other instances in which illegal immigrants have committed heinous crimes in America.

Sanctuary Cities Set a Bad Example by Flouting the Law

America has traditionally been a nation of laws. Being called a law-abiding citizen is high praise for an American. Consequently, when cities, counties, and states blatantly flaunt the law, they set the wrong example for their citizens, particularly youngsters. One of the veterans interviewed for this book asked how parents in sanctuary cities are supposed to impress on their children the importance of obeying the law when city leaders openly and purposefully flaunt the law. Good question.

Sanctuary cities are lawbreakers. Since 1996, federal law has mandated that local and state authorities must cooperate with federal agencies by sharing information about illegal immigrants. Disobeying this law is bad public policy. The unwritten rule in America has always been this: *If you don't like a law, change it; but until it is changed, obey it.* If cities, counties, and states can arbitrarily decide which laws to obey and which to ignore, why can't individual American citizens do the same? This raises an interesting question. If you get a parking ticket in a sanctuary city, should you pay it? After all, disobeying the law is public policy in sanctuary cities.

Sanctuary Cities Protect Illegal Immigrants Instead of Legal Citizens

City, county, and state leaders are elected to serve their citizens. Leaders of sanctuaries do just the opposite. They put protecting illegal immigrants ahead of protecting legal citizens. This means they are more concerned about people who come to America illegally and who immediately become a drain on government resources than about the tax-paying citizens who provide those resources. This is not just irresponsible; it's unconscionable. It's as if a burglar breaks into a house and decides to stay, and the owner treats the burglar better than he treats his own children.

Sanctuary Cities Increase Homelessness and the Problems Associated With It

Cities with large homeless populations face a number of challenges. Problems associated with homelessness include tent encampments intrusively erected in neighborhoods, car break-ins, smash-and-grab robberies, panhandling, trash in the streets, human waste on sidewalks, used needles tossed in the streets, rat infestations, and an increase in communicable diseases, to name just a few. One of the leading causes of diseases associated with the homeless is exposure to human waste. Business leaders in cities with large homeless populations complain constantly about their businesses being hurt because the homeless drive away customers.

Immigrants who enter the United States illegally just add to the number of homeless people living in the streets and, in turn, add to the problems associated with large homeless populations. Since sanctuary cities are natural destinations for illegal immigrants, these cities are experiencing an increase in their homeless populations. For example, the homeless population in San Francisco—a sanctuary city—rose by 16.8 percent between 2017 and 2019. In response, the mayor of San Francisco proposed spending $384 million to combat the problems associated with homelessness. That is a lot of money that could be spent on other pressing needs in the city if the homeless population were not growing so rapidly.

In his first budget after taking office in 2019, the governor of California, Gavin Newsom, proposed to spend $1 billion on homelessness. Again, that is a lot of money that could have gone toward solving some of California's many pressing problems. While hundreds of homes of legal California citizens are destroyed every year by mudslides and wildfires, California's governor is siphoning off public funds to alleviate homelessness while encouraging sanctuaries that increase the homeless population. Again, the twisted logic of socialists can be difficult to follow. Since porous borders allow a continual flow of illegal immigrants into the United States, and since these illegal immigrants are naturally drawn to sanctuary cities, other areas choosing to designate themselves as sanctuaries face the same kinds of challenges being faced in California. One can only wonder how long it will be before the tax-paying citizens of these cities and states tire of the problems and say "enough is enough."

Berkeley, California, has been a sanctuary city since the Vietnam War. Although Berkeley has long been known for its liberal policies, some of its citizens are finally saying "enough is enough." Businesses and everyday citizens in Berkeley are becoming increasingly disenchanted because of the problems caused by the homeless population, a population that will only grow as illegal immigrants seek sanctuary there. Responding to complaints, the city council decided to ban people from living in decrepit recreational vehicles. The move caused a firestorm.

A Veteran Speaks Out

"Conservatives need to educate all Americans concerning the chaos that is happening in European countries because of lax border security and open borders. Open borders would present our nation with a financial burden we could not endure. City officials in sanctuary cities who protect illegal immigrants instead of their own citizens should be put in jail. I believe sanctuary cities will eventually go away, because fed-up citizens who live in these cities will demand it."

—GEORGE FOUNTAS, *U.S. Air Force, 1974–1983*

Fountas spent most of his time in the Air Force serving in the Strategic Air Command (SAC). He exited the Air Force as an NCO and immediately went to work as a civil servant in aircraft maintenance and refueling, a field in which he served for thirty years.

Surrounding cities feared their homeless populations would increase as the Berkeley ban drove out homeless people. Also, old-line liberal diehards in Berkeley decried the ban. But businesses continued to pressure city leaders to do something. The citizens and leaders of other sanctuary cities are going to face the same kinds of intractable problems as illegal immigrants swell the ranks of their homeless populations. Then there is the issue of diseases.

As homeless populations grow in sanctuary cities, diseases long thought to be under control or eradicated in the United States are being reintroduced. Cities with large homeless populations are now dealing with a resurgence of typhus, tuberculosis, and other communicable diseases in homeless shelters and tent encampments. The threat of a bubonic plague outbreak is no longer just a science fiction plot twist. It is once again real.

As illegal immigrants settle in the shelters and tent camps of sanctuary cities, the likelihood of an increase in infectious diseases is magnified. To make matters worse, homeless encampments are often soaked in urine and littered with rotting trash, human waste, and used needles. Attracted by the filth, rats are drawn there, and rats help spread diseases. These circumstances represent a perfect storm when it comes to the outbreak of infectious diseases.

Homelessness was already sapping the resources of large cities before many of them chose to become sanctuaries for illegal immigrants. Now, with their homeless populations being increased by illegal immigrants seeking sanctuary, these cities are finding their progressive views challenged by common sense. As the leaders of the city of Berkeley, California, are learning, misguided good intentions can lead to unexpected bad consequences.

CHAPTER 7

Cultural Coarsening

The premise: "*Boundaries are a good indication of a God-honoring society—boundaries not just physical but cultural as well. I am a pastor and a retired Navy chief petty officer with more than twenty years of active service. I have been surrounded by sailors most of my adult life and have known men who could not complete a sentence without using profanity. It is one thing for that kind of language to be used on a ship full of sailors, but it is a mark of a declining culture when we hear high school children, homemakers, and neighbors using it in everyday discourse.*"

—AL STOUT, *pastor, U.S. Navy, 1985–2005*

The veteran who expresses the premise for this chapter is Pastor Al Stout. Pastor Stout served in the Navy for more than twenty years. Since retiring, he has continued to work for the Navy in a civilian capacity in information warfare training while also serving as a pastor. His service in the Navy took him to many different parts of the world and allowed him to serve several different churches. He was licensed to preach by First Southern Baptist Church of San Diego and ordained by Harmony Ridge Baptist Church in Pace, Florida. Pastor Stout and his wife, Mary, have four children and ten grandchildren.

Normalization of Coarseness

Our featured veteran for this chapter, Pastor Stout, made an important point about the crude language so common in America today. He said it is one thing to hear that kind of language on a ship full of sailors who, while at sea, are segregated from society, but quite another to hear it used in everyday conversation as if it were normal and acceptable. A lot of the veterans we interviewed and surveyed agreed with Pastor Stout.

One veteran who responded to our survey was deeply upset by what she saw as the coarsening of America's culture. This veteran wondered what has become of civility, human decency, and respect for human life in our country. The things she sees happening on nightly news programs take her back to those turbulent times in the antiwar era of the 1960s when she joined the military. In her comments, she wrote about recently being the victim of a particularly disturbing manifestation of cultural coarsening: road rage.

This veteran is not alone in being concerned about the crudeness, lack of decorum, incivility, poor manners, lack of respect for human life, and spiritual bankruptcy permeating the culture these days. Recently, there was a newspaper story about a mother who callously tossed her unwanted baby into a dumpster and another about an elementary schoolteacher who punished well-mannered students for saying "yes ma'am" to her. This teacher claimed to be offended by her students' politeness.

The ongoing coarsening of the culture is a fact of life in America today, and it affects all of us. People react to cultural decline in different ways. Some wring their hands in despair and wonder, "How did this happen?" Others, convinced America is rushing headlong over a moral cliff, feel helpless to stop it, so they respond out of anger and frustration. Americans who despair over the coarsening of our culture are both right and wrong. They are right to be concerned about the declining state of the culture, but they are wrong to think nothing can be done.

One veteran from our survey was adamant that not only can something be done, but it is everyday Americans—not elected officials and judges—who must do it. All Americans, according to this veteran, have an important role to play in reclaiming the culture. To this veteran, standing on the sidelines wringing one's hands in despair while the culture declines is unacceptable. He stated it is irresponsible to complain about the coarsening of the culture unless you are prepared to do something about it.

A Veteran Speaks Out

"The great societies that went before us—the Greeks, Babylonians, and Romans—all self-destructed because of moral failure. We are becoming so self-absorbed that we think we can succeed where these once great civilizations failed, and we can do it without God. This is folly in the extreme. Man has always needed an absolute standard so that people may live in peace. When we turn our backs on God, we cannot help but come to the same end as previous civilizations."

—*Robb Schiefer, U.S. Air Force, 1978–1982*

Schiefer served as a munitions specialist, loading munitions on F-4, F-106, and F-101 aircraft. After leaving the Air Force, he became a successful businessman, entrepreneur, restaurant owner/operator, and career coach.

Using the parable of the ten minas, another veteran interviewed for this book explained his view that we are to occupy
until the Lord returns (Luke 19:13). By "occupy," Christ means
we are to be good stewards of the world He gave us. It follows
then that Christ expects us to do all we can to make sure the
prevailing culture honors His Father. According to this veteran,
you don't honor God by sitting on the sidelines complaining or
impotently wringing your hands. God expects us to reclaim the
culture for Christ.

The role of all Americans in reclaiming the culture involves
reaching out to those whose behavior is unacceptable and
showing them a better way, one individual at a time. Some
people want to fight back by leading protest marches, organizing huge rallies, and raising money for political candidates.
These are all appropriate strategies for helping reclaim the
culture, but remember this important point: Reclaiming the
culture requires changing the hearts of those whose behavior
darkens it. Protest marches, rallies, and political debates rarely
change hearts, but individuals who set an example of living
according to Christian principles and traditional American
values can. Setting a good example that shows people a better
way speaks louder than protest rallies and marches.

Things may look dark to you, but there is no need to
despair; you can help change the hearts of those whose attitudes
and behavior coarsen the culture. You do it by engaging them
one-on-one in a positive manner. If everyone who is concerned
about cultural coarsening reaches out to just one person and
shows him or her a better way, the ongoing cultural decline
concerning so many Americans can be stopped in its tracks.
On the other hand, silence on the part of good people will just
accelerate the culture's decline.

The veteran who raised this issue in his response to our survey claimed the silence of good people is why the culture has declined. He stated his opinion in the firmest terms that good people who don't take a stand against bad behavior are guilty of condoning that behavior. This veteran even backed up his opinion with Scripture. He quoted James 4:17, which tells us that knowing the right thing to do but not doing it is a sin. He encouraged all Americans to reach out, stand up, and speak out when they see behavior that coarsens the culture.

Behaviors Coarsening the Culture

We do not claim coarse behavior is a new phenomenon. In fact, the opposite is true. One veteran we talked with made the point that destructive behavior has been with us since the dawn of history; it was introduced in the Garden of Eden and has been with us ever since. Never forget, the first murder known to man occurred when Cain killed his brother Abel (Genesis 4:1–16). The point to grasp here is this: The behaviors currently darkening the culture are not new. What is new is these behaviors have become so common and widespread. Worse yet, in some cases, they are now accepted as normal.

We have witnessed instances of cultural coarsening all throughout our lives. You probably have too. For example, there were school shootings many years ago when we were children—not many, but a few. There were also other forms of coarse behavior, including sexual abuse, incivility in public discourse, profanity, and workplace violence. But there are important differences between what happened in the past and what is happening now. The differences are found in the frequency of these behaviors and, worse yet, society's increasing acceptance of them.

Behaviors once thought deplorable or at least socially taboo are becoming not just commonplace but acceptable. Even the more extreme behaviors, such as mass shootings and workplace violence, though still unacceptable, have become less shocking because they happen so often. As a society, we are becoming inured to the ugly side of human nature. Unfortunately, this is what happens when people remain silent in the face of behaviors that should be challenged and rejected.

Crude behavior occurred as an exception in the past but now happens so often, it is becoming the rule. In many cases, behavior that in the past was considered repulsive no longer even raises eyebrows. One veteran who responded to our survey commented that when he was a youngster, men used to indulge their lust by surreptitiously subscribing to Hugh Hefner's prurient publication. Now all they have to do to view that kind of pornography is walk past the display window of a lingerie store in the local mall, watch prime-time television, or look at the ads in the morning newspaper. Worse yet, what they see, their children see. This veteran was concerned about the effect this kind of exposure was having on young boys, and wondered if it had anything to do with the rampant sexual abuse occurring in America.

Let's consider some of the behaviors contributing to the coarsening of America's culture. Here is a list of the ones pointed out by veterans who responded to our survey:

- Incivility
- Road rage
- Mass shootings
- Workplace violence
- Rudeness and incivility

- Rampant drug abuse

- Epidemic cheating

- Internet "flaming"

- Ubiquitous profanity

- Sexually explicit advertising

- Gratuitous violence on television, in movies, and in computer games

- In-your-face boasting in sports

- Sideline rage

This list of behaviors is illustrative but not comprehensive. These are just the ones pointed out most frequently by veterans who responded to our survey. You can probably add to the list. Let's examine these various contributors to cultural coarsening in more detail.

Road Rage

Drivers' becoming angry and behaving badly are hardly new phenomena. A veteran interviewed for this book told of an incident he remembered from his childhood. Two drivers got at cross purposes and hurled insults and epithets at each other. But nothing more than a few cross words ever came of the incident. In fact, the two angry drivers, realizing the foolishness of their behavior, burst out laughing, shook hands, and waved at each other as they drove off. But these days, peaceful outcomes such as this are less common. Instead, angry drivers are demonstrating a complete lack of self-restraint and acting out in destructive ways.

During the development of this book, a story made the news about a man who became angry because a woman was driving too slowly to suit him. The woman turned out to be a grandmother who was taking extra care because she was transporting her new grandchild. In a fit of impatience and anger, the man pulled up beside her car and fired a handgun into it. He missed the grandmother but killed the child. This kind of deplorable, tragic incident is much different from a couple of drivers exchanging angry words and then driving off in a huff. Unfortunately, violent road rage incidents like this are becoming common.

What makes this kind of incident especially disturbing is what it says about the human condition. This angry driver was willing to kill another person, a little baby, rather than wait the few seconds necessary before he could pass the grandmother's car. What could possibly be so important in this man's life that a delay of a few seconds would be worth killing a baby? How could a person be so lacking in self-restraint and humanity that a minor annoyance would lead him to engage in such deplorable behavior? These are the kinds of questions that concern not just veterans but a lot of other Americans too.

Unfortunately, incidents such as this are no longer rare. They aren't even exceptions. In fact, they are becoming the rule. Violent road rage incidents have become a frequent occurrence, and they often involve firearms or other deadly weapons. For example, more than 65 percent of traffic fatalities now result from angry, aggressive driving. Almost 40 percent of these fatalities involve a firearm. Close to half of the drivers who are victims of road rage respond with rage of their own, adding fuel to a fire already out of control.[50] Road rage is a national scourge darkening our culture.

Mass Shootings

The veterans who responded to our survey were especially disturbed by the rising tide of mass shootings, particularly school shootings. One veteran we surveyed claimed the worst violence happening when he was in school was guys fighting over girls. In researching this topic, we chose a year from our childhood, 1950, and checked to see if there were any school shootings that year. As it turned out, there was one—just one. It happened in New York City during a high school dance.

The shooting was the result of a disagreement between a student and a former classmate. In fact, a more accurate portrayal of this incident would be a shooting that happened to occur at a school rather than a school shooting in the contemporary sense of the term. Had the dance been held at another location, the shooting would have occurred there. In other words, the location was not a determining factor in the shooting, as it typically is with today's school shootings and other mass shootings occurring in malls, nightclubs, and other crowded locations. The shooter wasn't bent on producing maximum casualties, as is typically the case in contemporary mass shootings. Rather, he was angry at one person and wanted to settle a score with that person alone.

Unlike the incident in New York City in 1950, shooters today are choosing schools, malls, nightclubs, and other crowded locations because they are soft, accessible targets lending themselves to mass casualties. Since 2015, America has averaged twenty-four mass shootings per year. Vengeance, settling scores, acting on grievances, and the desire to kill as many people as possible are often the motives in today's mass shootings. The incident in New York City in 1950 was an exception, but the mass shootings of today are not. They occur too frequently to any longer be considered exceptions.

Workplace Violence

Workplace violence is not new, but the nature of the concept has changed radically in recent years. Retail businesses have long had to cope with criminals resorting to violence when breaking in and committing robbery. In fact, one of the most dangerous occupations in America is convenience store clerk, especially on the late-night shift. But convenience store clerk doesn't top the list of the most dangerous occupations.

That dubious distinction goes to emergency medical personnel. They top the list when it comes to being attacked on the job, typically by angry or out-of-control patients. But this kind of workplace violence is not new. Healthcare professionals understand that dealing with distraught patients who become aggressive is an occupational hazard and always has been.

What most concerned the veterans who responded to our survey are two increasingly common manifestations of workplace violence: 1) angry employees shooting their coworkers and supervisors, and 2) domestic abuse brought to the workplace. The latter happens when angry spouses choose the workplace as the setting for domestic confrontations. In fact, workplace violence is the second leading cause of death for women on the job. Workplace violence has become such a problem for employers the Occupational Safety and Health Administration (OSHA), a federal agency responsible for promoting on-the-job safety, has developed workplace-violence guidelines to help employers protect their personnel.

The veterans who commented on workplace violence have good reason to be concerned. The numbers are staggering.

Every year, almost two million people are victims of workplace violence in America. Homicides account for almost 10 percent of workplace deaths. Astonishingly, there are almost thirty thousand occurrences of rape and sexual assault in the workplace every year.[51] Each new instance of workplace violence coarsens the culture even more.

Incivility in Public Discourse

Several of the veterans who responded to our survey expressed concern about the lack of civility in everyday discourse. One veteran told of sitting in a restaurant having a meal while a woman at the table next to him talked loudly on her cell phone. He claimed everyone in the restaurant could hear the woman's side of the conversation, and although most of the other patrons were glaring at her in annoyance, this woman either didn't notice or didn't care.

Later that day, this same veteran was coming out of a grocery store. He held the door open for a young man who was juggling an armload of groceries. When the young man passed by without saying "thank you" or even acknowledging the courtesy, this veteran said, "You're welcome." The young man simply walked on, oblivious to his own rudeness. Had their roles been reversed, this veteran doubted if the young man would have bothered to open the door for him. He claimed people like this rude young man are so self-absorbed, they are blind to the needs of others.

A number of veterans commented on the practice of texting. How many times have you seen a car drifting into the wrong lane because the driver was texting? People who text while driving are willing to risk causing an automobile accident—possibly even fatalities—to read or send an inconsequential message that could and should have waited until they were parked. One-fourth of all automobile accidents are now caused by texting drivers. Cell phone use while driving—texting or talking on the phone—causes more than 1.5 million automobile accidents annually.[52]

Then there are those who text during meetings at work, classes at school, or in other settings where the practice is inappropriate, intrusive, or rude. This has become such a problem some businesses have designated certain meeting rooms as "no cell phone zones." Some schools have done the same thing with classrooms. One veteran said his personal pet peeve about texting is the driver who causes you to sit through a red light twice because he becomes so engrossed in texting he doesn't notice when the light turns green. Then, as he dashes through the yellow light at the last minute, you are left sitting through the red light again.

Rampant Drug Abuse

A veteran who responded to our survey commented that he cannot understand why so many people seek solace from their problems in drugs. Having joined the Army during the late 1960s, when marijuana became a symbol for those who refused to serve in the military, he finds it difficult to accept that states are now legalizing its use. According to this veteran, America is reaping what it has sown. Statistics support his contention. More than twenty-five million people misuse illegal or prescription drugs every year. Add to these the over sixty-seven thousand people who die annually from drug overdoses, the majority from opioid abuse, and the numbers are staggering.[53]

The United States spends more on healthcare than any other nation in the world yet ranks only twenty-seventh in life expectancy. In fact, the life expectancy of Americans is actually declining in some sectors, due primarily to drug and alcohol abuse. Among the many problems they cause, drug abuse and alcohol abuse are major contributors to the high suicide and crime rates in the United States. A veteran who works in the prison system commented that if drug abuse could somehow be eliminated, 80 percent of the prisoners he houses would not be incarcerated.

According to this veteran, who is now a corrections official, it is not just the use and sale of drugs increasing the inmate population nationwide. Drugs are the cause of many other crimes leading to prison sentences (for example, robbery, home invasions, theft, human trafficking, and prostitution). Securing drugs or the money to purchase them often leads to criminal activity. Further, drug deals gone bad are a leading cause of violent crimes, including murder.

The opioid crisis, as it has been labeled by the media, is the result of a sharp increase in the misuse of opioid drugs, prescription and illegal. Opioid drugs are painkillers that have a sedative effect on the body. Some people use them to deal with physical pain, while others use them to deal with emotional pain. Regardless of why people use opioids, these drugs are powerfully addictive and easy to overdose on. Drug overdoses are now a leading cause of death for Americans under fifty years of age, and the majority of these deaths are caused by opioids.[54] The opioid crisis knows no class or social boundaries, nor does it discriminate. Its destructive effects cut a wide swath across all segments of American society.

Epidemic Cheating

A veteran who pursued a college degree after retiring from the Air Force commented on what occurred in a management class he took. This veteran was the "old man" in the class. The lesson in question was on the subject of corporate ethics and social responsibility. Students were given a scenario in which they could benefit substantially if they were willing to cheat. The students were assured they would not get caught. Although a lot of people would be hurt by their cheating, no one would ever know they cheated. After discussing the hypothetical case, students were asked to anonymously divulge if they would be willing to cheat to gain the supposed benefits.

The veteran was astounded when most of the students checked the box indicating they would cheat, provided they wouldn't get caught. These students had no qualms about cheating, moral or otherwise; they just didn't want to get caught. If the only reservation young people have about cheating is getting caught, we have a serious problem. When the veteran tried to argue against cheating on moral grounds, the younger students in his class just rolled their eyes and ignored him.

Have we become a society that accommodates cheating, that responds to it with a wink and a nod? Here are just a few examples of recent cheating scandals making the news:

- Psychiatrists were caught accepting substantial fees to falsely diagnose young people as having a learning disability so they would be allowed extra time when taking the SAT or ACT examination.

- Wealthy Hollywood actresses were caught bribing college officials to grant their children admission to prestigious universities.

- Researchers at a major university accepted lucrative grants to downplay the negative side effects of a new drug while overstating its benefits.

- An individual was caught falsely claiming to have an advanced degree when applying for a job.

- Executives admitted to regularly cheating in business-related golf matches.

- More than 120 students at Harvard University were caught cheating on a take-home test.

- In the Atlanta public school system, teachers and principals were caught in a cheating scandal in which eleven of the twelve teachers accused were convicted of tampering with grades on statewide standardized tests. The teachers involved were trying to improperly increase test scores so they and their schools would not be accused of substandard teaching.

These are just a few representative examples. To catalogue all the cheating scandals occurring in the United States in just one year would require a book the size of the Oxford English Dictionary. In fact, developing cheating-detection software has become a growth industry for entrepreneurs, who market their products to schools and colleges. These cheating scandals and the many others not mentioned here raise a troubling question: Does a culture of cheating now exist in the United States? It's a question worthy of debate, but there is no debating the fact cheating is darkening the culture.

Sexual Abuse

A veteran who responded to our survey was shocked to learn how many sexual predators lived within a mile of his home. His concern was for his granddaughter, who often visited him and played with other kids in the neighborhood. Sexual abuse is widespread in America, but it's not new; it has occurred in all eras. In fact, it has been with us since the dawn of time. Consequently, it is not the existence of the problem but the size and frequency.

To gain an appreciation for how widespread this problem has become, search the internet for "registered sex offenders." There are almost 750,000 registered sex offenders in the United States, and the number is growing. Keep in mind those who are registered are just the tip of the iceberg, the ones who got caught and convicted. There are many additional sexual predators getting away with their despicable deeds, at least for the time being. You can check for sex offenders in your neighborhood by searching the internet for "sex offenders near me," but be forewarned: The results can be disturbing.

Internet "Flaming"

If you want to find out how low people are willing to go when expressing their opinions, read the comments sent to bloggers and recorded on social media sites. When a veteran we talked with decided to offer her opinion on a topic being discussed on her favorite internet site, she was shocked by the vile, vitriolic, and mean-spirited responses she received. The practice is known as "flaming." Flaming consists of sending insulting, hostile, and profane comments over the internet. People who practice flaming are emboldened by the anonymity the internet provides. They are also desensitized to the hurt they often cause. Flamers say things over the internet that they would never say face-to-face, and in so doing pollute cyberspace with their venom. Internet flaming has contributed greatly to cultural coarsening in a relatively short period of time.

Ubiquitous Profanity

Both of us served in the Marine Corps, so we have heard our share of profanity. But to hear it used by middle school children, as it so frequently is these days, is disturbing. Several of the veterans who responded to our survey commented they often hear youngsters using profanity that would shock even the saltiest sailor. Worse yet, adults don't seem to be inclined to correct them anymore. The state of the language in today's culture is alarming.

Words once bleeped out are now heard regularly on television and even more frequently in everyday conversations. One of the main reasons movies are given ratings other than G or even PG is crude language. One veteran commented that when he hears youngsters walking past his house swearing as if that is a normal and acceptable way of speaking, he thinks of Psalm 19:14.

This is the psalm his third-grade teacher made him copy a hundred times after he blurted out an expletive his father had used in his presence. This verse from Psalm 19 is a prayer that one's words and thoughts will be acceptable to God. The kind of language that this veteran, when a youngster, mimicked in front of his teacher was so unacceptable back then, she soundly chastised not just him but his father too. She called his father and scolded him for using inappropriate language in front of a child. The father apologized profusely. This veteran wondered if the parents of today would apologize as his father did years ago or just tell the upset teacher to mind her own business. In fact, he doubted the teachers of today would even raise an eyebrow at the profanity.

Sexually Explicit Advertisements

Several of the veterans who responded to our survey were concerned about sexually explicit advertising. Advertising of women's undergarments and other accessories has become so explicit, it's a wonder the pornography industry hasn't gone out of business. Modesty seems to be a thing of the past. Sex sells. Consequently, advertisers have adopted it as a favorite marketing strategy. Because of this, we are confronted by seminaked women and men in suggestive poses everywhere we turn. They pop up on billboards, in magazines, on television, in the newspaper, and on the internet. You see them all the time. So do your kids. You might ignore them, but your kids don't.

Gratuitously exposing the most intimate parts of the human body coarsens the attitudes of young people toward personal privacy. Because they become accustomed to seeing the bodies of people—primarily women—exposed in advertisements, young people grow up thinking they have a right to see the unclothed bodies of women anytime they want. One veteran suggested there must be a connection between the ubiquitous nature of sexually explicit advertising and the rising tide of sexual abuse in America. His point is valid. The possible connection is too obvious to ignore.

Gratuitous Violence in Movies, on Television, and in Computer Games

You have probably heard the maxim "You are what you eat." A logical extension of this maxim is "You become what you watch." This is why Scripture warns us to focus on what is good, right, worthy, and uplifting (Philippians 4:8). One veteran from our survey made the point that it should come as no surprise, young people who are immersed in violent movies and computer games would come to view violence as normal and acceptable. Numerous studies suggest this is the case.

Counselors who work with teenagers are well aware young people who enjoy playing violent computer games are more likely to act out aggressively. This is precisely what is happening in today's culture. Youngsters spend hours watching violent content. Yet people still shake their heads in bewilderment when one of them becomes angry and acts out in a violent manner. These teenage shooters are doing what they have watched their "heroes" from television, movies, and computer games do all their lives. A caveat is in order here. Although the fact youngsters who become violent are often imitating their action heroes might explain their violence, it does not excuse it.

Purveyors of violence in movies, on television, and in computer games try to deny any connection between their productions and the violent behavior coarsening the culture, but such denials are the height of hypocrisy. Those who question the connection between violent entertainment and the violence permeating society either are in denial or simply don't care. We are all affected by the entertainment we indulge in, but this is particularly the case for youngsters in their formative years. Youngsters are as pliable as modeling clay. This is why it is so important to expose them to role models who are positive, uplifting, and helpful. Young people fed a steady diet of violent movies, computer games, and television shows are traveling down a one-way street to a bad place.

In-Your-Face Boasting in Sports

A veteran who responded to our survey told of a disturbing scene he observed at a pee-wee football game. His grandson was the quarterback for one of the teams. Keep in mind the players on both teams were children in elementary school. A kid on the opposing team scored a touchdown. After dancing and strutting in the end zone, this kid ran past the opponents' bench pointing his finger and yelling insults at the players. When the boy's coach chastised him, the kid's father rushed to his defense, claiming his son was just doing what he saw football players on television do, as if this excused the bad behavior.

Although imitating professional athletes who behave like children is no excuse for a real child to behave badly, the father's statement was at least partially true. The kid was imitating what he saw on television. This is too bad, since some athletes are poster boys for bad behavior. In-your-face, unsportsman-like conduct has become pervasive in today's coarse culture. Dancing in the end zone and outrageous posturing for the cameras became so widespread in the National Football League, the owners were forced to pass a regulation forbidding it. Now players who do these things in excess can bring penalties on their team.

Another veteran explained that when he played football and other sports as a youngster, good sportsmanship was more than just a virtue; it was an enforced expectation. In practice or games, for example, he was taught that when he knocked an opponent down, he should help him back up. Win or lose, after the game he and his teammates were expected to shake hands with opponents and say "good game." When they scored a touchdown, the coach expected his players to act like they had been in the end zone before. They were taught to quickly hand the ball to the referee and get ready for the kickoff—no dancing, no strutting, and no posturing for the crowd.

In an era when good sportsmanship was emphasized, the kind of behavior associated with some modern athletes would have brought the wrath of the entire coaching staff down on the boastful miscreants. Poor sportsmanship once could cause even the best athletes to suffer the indignation of being benched. This is no longer the case. During the writing of this book, the Little League World Series was aired. A youngster on a South American team scored a run. Before going into the dugout, he stood in front of the crowd and performed a crude, even vulgar, dance. His teammates and people in the stands applauded his poor sportsmanship and vulgarity.

The next day, television morning-show hosts aired his gyrating dance over and over, complimenting him for his youthful enthusiasm and calling it "cute." What nonsense. The kid should have been benched, and the pandering morning-show hosts should have been fired. Children learn lasting lessons by watching adults play the games they love. Unfortunately, the strutting, in-your-face antics seen so often in sports today teach young people the wrong lessons. Then when they are validated by other adults, like the morning-show hosts who thought the Little Leaguer's vulgar dance was cute, the culture is coarsened and the rest of us suffer.

Sideline Rage

A veteran from our survey said he played baseball and football from elementary school through college and in the military. There were always parents at the games who disagreed with umpires, referees, and coaches, and a few who hurled insults at them. But the other parents gave a wide berth to those who disparaged game officials. Nobody wanted to be associated with them. These ill-mannered parents, though loud and often obnoxious, were the exception, not the rule. The veteran who told this story could not remember even one instance of a parent attacking referees, coaches, umpires, or other parents during all his years of playing sports.

But in recent years, things have changed. Attacks on game officials, coaches, and parents during children's sports events have become so common, the phenomenon now has its own name: sideline rage. Here are just a few instances of sideline rage that have occurred in recent years. A parent poisoned the players on the opposing youth football team to help ensure her son's team would win the championship game. A father was beaten to death in front of children by another parent at a hockey game. A brawl broke out among parents at a Tee Ball game in front of four- and five-year-old kids. A dentist sharpened the face guard on his son's football helmet so the boy could slash opposing players (five players and the referee were injured). A parent paid a ten-year-old pitcher two dollars to purposely hit a batter during a Little League game.[55]

The list of sideline-rage incidents could go on, and it grows by the day, but you get the picture. Most instances of sideline rage involve fathers. However, increasingly mothers are joining the fray. Becoming violent over a referee's decision in a youth football or soccer game or over an umpire's call in a youth baseball game is bad enough, but what is worse is the lesson children learn from observing adults becoming enraged and acting out their emotions in violent ways. Out-of-control parents who commit acts of sideline rage—fathers and mothers—are teaching young, impressionable children that violence is an acceptable response when things don't go their way.

A Veteran Speaks Out

"When I see things like school shootings, workplace violence, drug abuse, and road rage, I worry about the world my grandchildren will grow up in."

—GREG WALDRON, *U.S. Army, 1984–1988*

Waldron left the Army as an NCO and has had a long career supporting the Air Force in test-range operations as a defense contractor.

Causes of Cultural Coarsening

Our values grow out of our most deeply held beliefs. They guide our attitudes, behavior, opinions, and decisions. One veteran from our survey made the valid point that as our values decline, the culture also declines. This is precisely what is happening in America. There are many contributing causes when it comes to the coarsening of America's culture, but there is only one root cause. The root cause is, as individuals and as a nation, we have strayed from our moral foundation and core values, values that grew out of the Judeo-Christian worldview. As a result, America is teetering on the edge of a moral cliff.

Those whose actions coarsen the culture are guided by self-indulgence, self-gratification, and a lack of self-discipline rather than the selflessness and self-control taught in Scripture. Unlike the secular humanists of today who reject Scripture and its Author, the founders understood there must be boundaries, absolutes, and definite rights and wrongs. They also understood man does not set these boundaries or establish the absolutes, nor is man the final arbiter of truth. These things are the purview of God, not man. This is why He gave us the Bible to serve as a guide in determining what is right and wrong and to reveal Himself as sovereign.

The founders were not moral relativists who believed "anything goes." Rather, they knew the truth comes from Scripture and a life lived in accordance with God's Word is a better life. This is not to say they did not occasionally stray from those beliefs. Of course they did. America's founders weren't perfect; no one is. The Bible speaks to this phenomenon. In Romans 7:19, the Apostle Paul bemoans the fact he fails to do the good things he wants to do and keeps doing the evil things he doesn't want to do. We all face this dilemma from time to time. It's part of our fallen nature.

The contributing causes of cultural coarsening are many, beginning with misguided and negligent parenting. Parents who fail to teach their children to respect other people, obey the rules, submit to rightful authority, and behave responsibly contribute to cultural decline. You cannot expect children to magically become responsible, contributing adults if they are not taught the importance of responsibility during their formative years.

Schools emphasizing self-esteem over self-discipline contribute to cultural decline, because poor self-control is a contributing factor in road rage, mass shootings, workplace violence, sideline rage, and other manifestations of cultural coarsening.

The entertainment industry's obsession with gratuitous sex and violence coarsens the culture and is used by Satan to destroy lives. Based on the content of movies and computer games, should we really be surprised when young people display a lack of respect for human life? Advertisers who encourage "me-ism" coarsen the culture too, because people who adopt an "it's all about me" attitude are not likely to show others courtesy, respect, or empathy.

There is no question parents, schools, and the entertainment industry are complicit in the coarsening of the culture. But there is one institution that contributes at least as much as any of them, and probably more. That institution is higher education. Few culturally influential institutions have contributed more to the coarsening of American culture or strayed so far from their moral roots and professed purposes than academia.

Colleges and universities in America have long held as their fundamental purpose the pursuit of truth, promotion of research and scholarship, transmission of knowledge, development of character and intelligence, and transformation of people into productive, contributing citizens who can function in a diverse, pluralistic, and democratic society. Sounds good, doesn't it? But there is a problem.

Many colleges and universities long ago stopped living up to these ideals. For example, the pursuit of truth has been replaced by indoctrination in the principles of progressive dogma. The truth as taught in colleges and universities today is a flexible concept theoretically determined by the individual, but in reality, it is determined by socialists masquerading as educators. To moral relativists, absolute truths do not exist and standards of right and wrong are passé. Socialists will claim there are no absolute rights or wrongs and then, with a straight face, insist they are absolutely right. The irony in their claim is blatantly obvious, yet socialists don't or won't see it.

This historical fact of America's educational founding on the Bible is an inconvenient truth many colleges and universities now cover up or deny. Institutions of higher education today typically reject traditional values, enforce political correctness, demean Christian students, and discourage or even punish conservative thinking.

Because the majority of college students enroll at an age when they are still impressionable and their minds and characters are malleable, colleges and universities are able to indoctrinate thousands of students every year and turn them into minions of the left. Worse yet, institutions of higher education have used their respected position in society to lend credibility to some of the worse perpetrators of cultural coarsening. It's as if our publicly funded universities are on a mission to kill the goose that continues to lay their golden egg. Once again, the illogic of the left is difficult to understand. The irony is deepened when you consider the excessive cost of this indoctrination dumped on the backs of the students and their parents in the form of debt.

By granting unworthy artists, musicians, and performers their imprimatur, colleges and universities lend credibility to work lacking even a hint of redeeming value. With the stamp of approval of colleges and universities, trash is being passed off on society as art, music, literature, and cinema. Then, anyone who questions the artistic value of this trash is portrayed as a boneheaded troglodyte and quickly becomes a target for the vitriol of progressive elitists.

By accepting the unacceptable and lending worth to the unworthy, colleges and universities have gone from enhancing the quality of life in America to poisoning it. In the name of tolerance, they pander to bad actors with nefarious agendas while refusing to tolerate Christians and conservatives. Whereas institutions of higher education were once considered exemplars of what is good, right, and worthy in society, many campuses now resemble zoos with all the cages left open. They are places where anything goes, and the more culturally coarse the activities the better. All the while, the value of a college education continues to decline while the costs continue to rise, costs that outpace by far the consumer price index. As a result, students are paying more for what degrades their lives and the lives of those around them.

What Are You Going to Do About It?

We understand the frustration veterans and other Americans feel concerning the coarsening of the culture. We are frustrated by this trend too. But while serving in the Marine Corps, we learned to confront challenges head-on and overcome obstacles with a can-do attitude, relentless determination, and steadfast perseverance. The most revered Marine in the corps' long and storied history is Chesty Puller, who commanded the 1st Marine Division at the Chosin Reservoir during the Korean War.

Puller and his Marines suddenly found themselves surrounded by thousands of Chinese soldiers and badly outnumbered when China, with no warning, entered the war on the side of North Korea. Embedded journalists, fearing for their lives, asked Colonel Puller what he planned to do. His response is instructive for Americans who feel impotent and frustrated when it comes to the ongoing cultural decline in America. It shows how a determined person with a can-do attitude approaches problems.

Puller calmly told the journalists that he had been searching for enemy soldiers for days. Now that he and his Marines were surrounded, they would have no problem finding and defeating them. Puller's approach to what others saw as an insurmountable problem is the one we recommend to veterans and all other Americans who respect the values that made our country great. Rather than fretting about the coarsening of the culture, we recommend you adopt Chesty Puller's approach, look at the declining culture as a challenge, and start doing something about it.

Throughout history, whenever a nation has gone astray in ways that shock the senses, those who later have the benefit of hindsight always ask the same question: Why didn't somebody do something? For example, in the aftermath of the Holocaust, this question was asked repeatedly. Historians still puzzle over it. Why didn't somebody do something when it became obvious Hitler and his Nazi minions were bent on exterminating an entire people? Why didn't someone speak up when thousands of Jews were rounded up, stuffed into train cars, and sent to death camps?

Several reasons have been suggested, with apathy, fear, and self-preservation being the most frequent. Regardless the reasons, what cannot be denied is despite some laudable and courageous exceptions, a lot of good people knew bad things were happening and did nothing. This brings to mind an often-quoted statement: "All that is necessary for the triumph of evil is that good men do nothing." This statement is usually attributed to Edmund Burke, but scholars are unable to pin down its source. Regardless of whom the author happens to be, the statement is prescient. This is why we ask people who are wringing their hands in despair over the declining state of America's culture, "What are you going to do about it?"

This is not a frivolous question, nor is it intended to be insensitive. Those who are Christians understand we will all stand in judgment one day (Romans 14:10–13). These verses from Romans make clear we will all have to give an account of ourselves. When that day comes, it is quite possible we will be asked what we did about the decline of America's culture. Did we just stand by impotently fretting, or did we stand up, speak out, and show others a better way? This is what God expects us to do.

God does not want us to despair, fret, or fume, nor does He want us to raise a white flag and give up. Rather, in an era of cultural decline, He wants us to shine the light of Christ into the darkest recesses of America's culture. He expects you and me to do our part to reclaim the culture for Him, one misguided American at a time. Like Chesty Puller and his Marines at the Chosin Reservoir, those of us who believe in the original vision of the founders are surrounded by determined opponents who reject this vision. When confronted by these opponents, don't back up even an inch from what you know to be the truth. Instead, stand up and speak out.

CHAPTER 8

Anti-Christian, Anticonservative Bias in Higher Education and the Media

The premise: "I find it difficult to understand why opposing points of view are often not tolerated at our country's institutions of higher learning. As a retired combat-wounded Navy veteran, I understand the importance of and sacrifice required to protect the freedoms we Americans enjoy—freedoms that do not exist in many parts of the world today. Yet since my retirement in 2014, it appears that some of these freedoms are being slowly restricted, at least for those conservatives who seek to have a voice on left-leaning campuses. I consider my own service to be, in part, about fighting so that protections offered by the First Amendment can be fully enjoyed by all Americans. It is hard to comprehend a liberal orthodoxy that seems to become ever more pervasive on many college and university campuses that would restrict the right of freedom of expression to only those who concur with that orthodoxy. The most logical place for the free expression and exchange of ideas should be on the campuses of colleges and universities. Intolerance of conservative voices and opinions not only conflicts with our country's constitutional protections and values, but serves poorly the free exchange of ideas that has long been a hallmark of America's institutions of higher learning. Further polarization based on lack of discourse and the sharing of ideas is the last thing this country should tolerate. The suppression of ideas, no matter which side of the political spectrum it comes from, is not why many of us fought for this country."

—*JOHN R. "JACK" CAPRA, J.D., Ph.D., U.S. Navy, 1992–2014*

The veteran who expresses the premise for this chapter is Captain Jack Capra. Captain Capra earned his undergraduate degree from Florida State University in 1989 and went on to earn his law degree (J.D.) in 1992 from St. Thomas University College of Law. Following law school, he continued his education, earning four master's degrees and a doctorate degree in Christian studies (Columbia Evangelical Seminary, 2014). He served on active duty with the Navy from 1992 to 1997, during which time his duties included being assistant force judge advocate for the 5th Fleet at Bahrain and force judge advocate for Operation Deep Freeze in Antarctica.

Captain Capra transitioned to the Naval Reserves in 1997. However, he was called back to active service on six occasions following the terrorist attacks of September 11, 2001. While serving in Basra, Iraq, in 2004, Capra was wounded when enemy insurgents detonated a radio-controlled IED under his military convoy. He was awarded a Purple Heart and a Combat Action Ribbon for his service in Basra. As a civilian, Capra has enjoyed a successful career serving as a practicing attorney, an elected official, and a government relations council member for a state college.

ANTI-CHRISTIAN, ANTICONSERVATIVE BIAS IN HIGHER EDUCATION

Our featured veteran for this chapter, Captain Capra, made an important point about higher education as an institution in America. Anti-Christian and anticonservative bias on the campuses of colleges and universities runs counter to the very purpose of these institutions. If there is anywhere in America where the free exchange of ideas should be encouraged and welcomed, it is on the campuses of colleges and universities.

America was born out of war in 1776 and has fought in many more wars since George Washington and his ragtag troops gallantly led our country to independence. But perhaps the most important war Americans have fought since our War of Independence is not World War II, the Cold War, or even the war on terrorism. It's the one being waged inside our country every day, a war against the founders' vision and the core values that made America great. This is a battle for the very soul of America, a battle not of guns and missiles but of ideas. Two of the main battlegrounds in this epic confrontation are college and university campuses and the mainstream media. We begin with colleges and universities.

As mentioned several times previously, colleges and universities in America were once leading proponents of Christian thought and traditional values, but over time they have morphed into hotbeds of leftist indoctrination and progressive antipathy toward the America envisioned by our founders. As one of the veterans interviewed for this book stated, conservatives and Christians are about as welcome in colleges and universities as a mother-in-law on a honeymoon. Many of America's colleges and universities should erect signs at the front gate emblazoned with "Christians and Conservatives Not Wanted."

Ironically, the tactics employed by socialists in conducting their assault on Christianity, conservatism, and traditional American values violate the very principles which they claim to believe. The guerilla tactics used by progressive professors violate the principles of free speech, free thought, and free inquiry that have long been sacrosanct in higher education and are supposedly protected by academic freedom. Academic freedom, in turn, is supposed to be the philosophical cornerstone of higher education in America.

Unfortunately, on too many college and university campuses, academic freedom applies only to those who toe the line of progressive orthodoxy. Students are free to say and think what they want as long as it comports with the anti-Christian, anticonservative narrative of progressivism. Other views are not only unwelcome but belittled, attacked, and suppressed. God help the student who mentions biblical creation in a biology class or a professor who joins the Republican Party.

Way back in 2002, Phyllis Schlafly wrote an article titled "Diversity Dishonesty on College Campuses." Her article was accurate at the time, and is even more accurate today. Things have actually gotten worse since Schlafly made the valid point that diversity, multiculturalism, and tolerance as practiced on university campuses are shams. Politically correct socialists have redefined and weaponized these words to support their left-wing agenda. Further, what is deemed politically correct is determined by socialists. To be politically correct is to toe the line of progressive orthodoxy. Multiculturalism means accepting all cultures except the Judeo-Christian culture. Tolerance means accepting anything socialists deem appropriate and rejecting anything they don't.[56]

To appreciate how far institutions of higher education have strayed from their traditional mission, consider how writer David Horowitz describes that mission. Horowitz lists the purposes of higher education as the pursuit of truth; uncovering new knowledge through research; the critical but reasoned study of intellectual and cultural traditions; teaching and learning; preparing students for successful, contributing lives in a pluralistic democracy; and the transmission of knowledge.[57] This is certainly a worthy mission, but it's a mission that cannot be accomplished without an unwavering commitment to academic freedom, freedom of speech, and freedom of inquiry, a commitment that no longer exists.

Most colleges and universities still publicly profess purposes at least similar to those listed by Horowitz, but the gap between their claims and reality makes the Grand Canyon look like a drainage ditch. With some rare but commendable exceptions, progressive propaganda and leftist indoctrination are the new normal in higher education. Not surprisingly, most progressive academicians deny this assertion. This being the case, here are a few questions one might reasonably ask these naysayers:

- If the pursuit of truth is one of your purposes, why do you limit or suppress scholarly inquiry that might challenge your preconceived notions?

- If discovering new knowledge is one of your purposes, why do you either ignore or attack research supporting intelligent design?

- If the study and reasoned criticism of intellectual and cultural traditions is one of your purposes, why is your criticism a one-way street? Why are the ideas of Christians and conservatives suppressed and punished rather than fairly and openly debated?

- If helping students become productive citizens of a pluralistic democracy is one of your purposes, why are Christians and conservatives not included in your vision of pluralism?

- If free inquiry and free speech are essential to achieving your purposes, why do you suppress them?

- If you truly believe your secular humanist views are valid, why are you afraid to hear other points of view? People who are unwilling to give an objective hearing to differing points of view have no faith in the validity of their own views.

Compare the traditional purposes of higher education with the realities on college and university campuses today. Here are some of the favorite tactics of progressive administrators and faculties for suppressing the thoughts, speech, ideas, and avenues of inquiry of Christian and conservative students and professors:[58]

- Making derogatory comments in front of other students and colleagues about their work and beliefs.

- Refusing to award them degrees and denying them admission to graduate school if they reject Darwinian evolution or support the concept of intelligent design.

- Denying promotions to professors who refuse to toe the line of progressive orthodoxy.

- Censoring literature that's critical of progressive orthodoxy by controlling which books and periodicals are made available in college and university libraries.

- Denying tenure to and even terminating the contracts of professors who refuse to toe the line of progressive orthodoxy.

- Demoting and reassigning tenured professors who refuse to toe the line of progressive orthodoxy.

- Threatening and intimidating Christian and conservative speakers who are invited to speak on their campuses (although this is becoming less common, because Christians and conservatives are rarely invited to speak at colleges and universities anymore).

How Socialists View Christians and Conservatives

It is difficult for those outside academia to understand how virulent the left's attacks on Christians and conservatives can be and how deeply felt their animosity is. People often have a Disney World view of what takes place on the campuses of colleges and universities. They tend to view these institutions as places where diverse points of view are welcomed, and where bright people debate their differing opinions in a supportive and collegial environment, disagreeing without being disagreeable. In other words, they think the scholarly environment in higher education is what it is supposed to be and what socialists claim it is. When provided actual examples to the contrary, people unaffiliated with colleges and universities are often shocked.

As an example of how socialists view Christians and conservatives, Peter Singer, a bioethics professor from Princeton

University, claimed there are three possibilities when it comes to God: 1) God exists but does not care about the problems of people, 2) God cares about the struggles of people but is unable to do anything about them, or 3) God doesn't exist. Singer made it clear that the last possibility is his choice.[59]

A Veteran Speaks Out

"As a college professor for more than thirty-five years, I am disappointed to see reports of Christian and conservative speakers shouted down when they are invited to speak at colleges and universities. Worse yet, they are seldom invited to speak in the first place. This is the opposite of what should happen in institutions of higher education. Our colleges and universities are supposed to be bastions of free speech and diversity of thought, and these things are supposed to fall under the protective umbrella of academic freedom. By turning to politically correct groupthink tactics and refusing to hear anything but the party line of progressives, colleges and universities have sold their souls. I fear higher education is going to suffer an eventual death from the trauma of a self-inflicted wound."

—RAYMOND L. RICKMAN, U.S. Air Force, 1975–1982

Rickman left the Air Force as an NCO, completed college and graduate school, and had a long and successful career as a college professor.

Sentiments such as Singer's are not limited to the faculty members of Ivy League institutions. The faculties of many of our state institutions are now dominated by leftist professors who share Singer's views. Professor Steven Weinberg of the University of Texas called religion a nice dream but went on to say it's time we all woke up from it.[60] In a letter to the editor, *Free Inquiry* reader John Indo suggested that religious fundamentalists be required to take a class in logic, but then opined it would probably do no good because their minds are too limited. He went on to state that the far religious right had to be stopped, no matter the cost.[61]

Indo's statement summarizes accurately and concisely the agenda of the radical left. It is not sufficient to just ridicule, persecute, and intimidate Christians and conservatives; they must be stopped at all costs. In other words, it does not matter what socialists have to do to stamp out Christianity; they should do whatever it takes. As should be clear from these few quotes, the radical left is waging war on Christians, they intend to win that war, and they are willing to do anything, no matter how scurrilous, to emerge victorious.

The Radical Left's Attacks on Campus Freedoms

Examples of attacks on campus freedoms by the radical left are abundant. One of the best sources for this kind of information is Alliance Defending Freedom (ADF), an organization that defends Christians and conservatives who are being persecuted for their beliefs. To get a feel for how widespread and frequent these attacks are, consider the following representative cases chronicled by ADF:[62]

Speech Codes

A university in New York established a speech code that on the surface appeared to do little more than encourage good manners, but the code is a wolf in sheep's clothing. The code made any speech in residence halls that is not courteous, polite, or mannerly impermissible. While universities may certainly establish codes of conduct to ensure the ability of students to sleep and study in dormitories, restricting all speech in a dormitory to that which is courteous, polite, and mannerly is just a surreptitious way of silencing the views of students and their ability to voice them. After all, who decides what is courteous, polite, and mannerly?

Socialists have a habit of describing any speech they don't agree with as hate speech. With such a speech code in place, any student who happens to voice disagreement with another student's lifestyle, behavior, or personal choices can be charged and disciplined; conservatives are likely to be the most frequent targets of speech code violations. In fact, it requires little logic to arrive at the conclusion that these speech codes are aimed specifically at Christian and conservative students to coerce them into politically correct conformance.

Manufactured Offense

A student employee at an Indiana university was charged with racial harassment for doing nothing more than reading the book *Notre Dame vs. the Klan: How the Fighting Irish Defeated the Ku Klux Klan.* The absurdity of the charge can be seen in the title of the book. The book chronicles events in which the University of Notre Dame stood up to the Klan, something it should be commended for doing. All students should be encouraged to read this book. Yet just having the words "Ku

Klux Klan" on the cover was enough to offend another student, who brought charges against the student employee.

Christian Speech Suppressed

A Christian was arrested and charged with trespassing after sharing his faith on the campus of a community college in Schenectady, New York. A student was speaking about his faith and distributing religious tracts in a public area of the campus, when the college's assistant dean told him to stop preaching and leave the campus or be arrested, a clear violation of the student's First Amendment rights.[63] The assistant dean's actions were also a violation of the supposed mission of institutions of higher education to encourage exposure of students to a wide range of opinions, thoughts, and ideas.

Christian Student Organization Banned

Officials at Shippensburg University in Pennsylvania used provisions in the institution's speech code to strip a Christian student organization of its rights and privileges. The reason given: The organization required members to honor a statement of faith, and it selected its leaders according to its interpretation of biblical teaching.[64]

Religious Discrimination

Two students at a Georgia university were subjected to religious discrimination for maintaining a biblical view of homosexuality, a view in violation of the university's "safe space" training program. The "safe space" program ridicules religions that do not embrace homosexuality.[65]

Christian Conversation Banned

A Christian at a Louisiana university was prevented from sharing his faith with other students. When this student tried to engage others in conversation about their faith at a location on campus designated for outside speakers, campus police intervened and informed him he needed a permit. University officials then informed the student his application for a permit had to be filed seven days in advance. If approved, he would be restricted to a two-hour block of time every seven days.

In order to apply, he would be required to pay a fee, divulge his Social Security number, and submit information about the content of his speech.[66] In other words, at this university, Christians are allowed freedom of speech only if they have a permit, only on certain days, only for certain amounts of time, only in selected locations, only if they pay a fee, and only if they are willing to divulge confidential personal information. One wonders if students at this university are required to read George Orwell's book *Nineteen Eighty-Four*.

Christian Men's Organization Banned

A Florida university refused to recognize a Christian fraternity, Beta Upsilon Chi, because it admitted only Christian men. However, the university permits other groups to limit their memberships according to specific criteria of their choosing.[67]

Religious and Conservative Statements Banned

A Pennsylvania university censored the religious and conservative views of a student who was a member of the Pennsylvania National Guard, claiming his views violated the school's speech code. He was prohibited from making religious and conservative statements in class and in conversations with other students.[68]

Pro-Life Group Segregated From Other Students

A Maryland university inhibited a pro-life group's efforts to share its message on campus. A student reserved space for the Rock of Life Club's Genocide Awareness Project, and permission was granted. The project was originally approved for display in front of the University Center, but permission was quickly rescinded by university officials, who required the club to move the display to a succession of different locations, each more isolated than the previous location. The final location was a vacant lot far removed from student traffic. In other words, Rock of Life was free to express its views provided it did so in a location where those views would not be heard.[69]

These examples are representative of what is taking place on college and university campuses nationwide. The radical left is persistent and increasingly aggressive in its attempts to silence Christian and conservative speech, thought, and inquiry. This is intellectual cowardice and academic tyranny at their worst.

Conservative Professors Not Allowed in Higher Education?

Few people familiar with higher education would deny the contention that most college and university professors lean far to the left. One of the veterans interviewed for this book told of applying for an adjunct (part-time) teaching position at a university. This veteran was highly qualified and taught at the Naval Academy. But when he was questioned about his views on various subjects, his conservatism became apparent. Not surprisingly, he was unceremoniously shown the door. He never heard back from the department chair who interviewed him.

A Veteran Speaks Out

"As moral relativism or situational ethics continues to be endorsed throughout American institutions of higher education, we can only expect incivility and other manifestations of moral ambiguity to continue. As responsible citizens, we are obliged to base our standards on proven foundations. It is essential that, beginning with the commander in chief, our decisions as a nation be based on our society's moral absolutes. For all of us, knowledge of right and wrong must be coupled with its active application. The New Testament book of James states: 'So whoever knows the right thing to do and fails to do it, for him it is sin' (James 4:17)."

—DAVID SWAN, *U.S. Navy, 1968–1991, and Robert Collins, U.S. Air Force, 1981–2009*

Swan served as a helicopter pilot, flying search-and-rescue missions (SAR) in Vietnam and antisubmarine warfare (ASR) missions during the Cold War. Collins served as an Air Force chaplain with two tours in Iraq and two tours in Afghanistan.

A recent study verified the assertion that higher education has become the almost exclusive domain of liberals. The study was conducted by Mitchell Langbert, an associate professor of business at Brooklyn College, and published by the National Association of Scholars; it revealed the ratio of registered Democrats to registered Republicans at fifty-one of the sixty-six top-ranked liberal arts institutions was 12.7 to 1, and that almost 40 percent of the colleges in the study had no registered Republicans on their faculties.[70]

The sample size for Langbert's study is impressive. The study included 8,688 tenure-track professors at fifty-one institutions of higher education. He found the ratio of Democrats to Republicans in the most common academic fields heavily favors Democrats, as shown by the following statistics:[71]

- Communications: 108 to 0 (no registered Republicans, which is particularly interesting in this area, which produces people going into media)
- Religion: 70 to 1
- Anthropology: 56 to 0
- English: 48 to 3.1
- Sociology: 43 to 8.1
- Art: 40 to 3.1
- Music: 32 to 8.1
- Theater: 29 to 5.1
- Classics: 27 to 3.1
- Geoscience: 27 to 1
- Environmental Science: 25 to 3.1
- Language: 21 to 1.1
- Biology: 20 to 8.1
- Philosophy: 17 to 5.1
- History: 17 to 4.1
- Psychology: 16 to 8.1
- Political science: 8 to 2.1

In only one academic field did the ratio favor Republicans over Democrats. That field is engineering, with a ratio of 6.1 Republicans for every Democrat. There is no question about who holds the reins of power in higher education. Liberals have gained control, and they are using the power of their numbers to maintain control, a fact allowing them to perpetuate their shameful approach to student development: teaching students *what* to think rather than *how* to think.

Consequences of Liberal Tyranny in Higher Education

In the previous section, we documented how lopsided college and university faculties are when it comes to political affiliation and, in turn, worldviews. The numerical dominance of liberals in colleges and universities is not an issue to be ignored. It has consequences for the long-term viability of higher education in this country and, more importantly, for the future of our nation. Here are just a few of the consequences resulting from the lack of balance on college and university faculties:

Research subjects are limited, and reports of the findings are biased.

Limiting research and scholarly inquiry to those topics liberal faculty members find acceptable undermines the discovery of new knowledge. This, in turn, undermines America's ability to maintain its historic position as the world's innovation leader in a variety of important fields. This is sad, because people all over the world have benefited immensely from the inventions and other innovations of American scientists and scholars. Here are just a few of those inventions: personal computers, mobile phones, the internet, the Global

Positioning System (GPS), lasers, microwave ovens, cardiac defibrillators, and hearing aids.

That our country is the world's leader in research, innovation, and scholarly inquiry can be seen in the fact that Americans lead other nationalities by far in receiving the Nobel Prize. As of this writing, there are 860 Nobel laureates. Of these, 375 are Americans. This puts our country well ahead of the second-place nation, the United Kingdom, which has 131 Nobel laureates. When institutions of higher education limit scholarly inquiry to that which advances the cause of progressive orthodoxy, America's position as the world's innovation leader is jeopardized. In a globally competitive world, the United States cannot afford to fall behind in the areas of innovation and entrepreneurship. Our standard of living depends on leading the world in these areas.

Freedom of thought and speech is suppressed, or at least inhibited.

The stifling of free speech and thought is a tragedy long associated with dictators on the right and left, not the United States of America, where free speech is supposed to be protected by the First Amendment. The Nazi thugs of Hitler's regime controlled what could be said and by whom, as did Castro in Cuba and a succession of communist dictators in the former Soviet Union. This was tyranny, and all these nations suffered because of it.

When college professors take it upon themselves to teach students what to think rather than how to think, they take a major step in the direction of tyranny. When they establish speech codes limiting what is said to what is deemed politically correct, they take another step. When they punish students and professors who refuse to obey the speech codes, they take the final step and have transformed their campuses into what one of the veterans interviewed for this book described as "academic gulags," in which the inmates (students) have to pay for the privilege of incarceration.

In his article "Free Speech and Its Present Crisis," historian Allen C. Guelzo makes the point that the right to express one's opinion in America today is threatened by liberal activists and authorities alike. According to Guelzo, in a Constitution Day speech at Princeton University, Professor Carolyn Rouse called free speech nothing more than a political illusion, a baseless scam to allow people to say anything they want. Rouse claimed there are different kinds of speech and not all of them should be protected by the First Amendment.[72] One might reasonably ask Rouse why, if she is correct, the founders did not see fit to include her exceptions in the First Amendment.

Her contention raises the critical question of who decides what speech should and should not be protected by the First Amendment. Just because Rouse and her fellow travelers in higher education find certain statements offensive does not negate the constitutional protections of the First Amendment for others. After all, the only kind of speech needing protection is offensive speech. Socialists who want to censor any and all speech they cannot control are little better than those misguided members of Congress in 1798 who passed the Alien and Sedition Acts. President John Adams lives again, but this time as a liberal Democrat.

The credibility of higher education is undermined.

Writing for *The Washington Times*, Jennifer Harper explored the effect liberal bias is having on the credibility of higher education in America. According to Harper, public confidence in higher education has taken a nosedive in recent years. She stated that college and university administrators have noticed the steady erosion of credibility and attribute it in part to liberal bias at their institutions.[73] According to Harper, approximately one-third of college administrators agree the American public views colleges as being intolerant of conservative views, and 51 percent agree institutions of higher education are out of touch with society. Interestingly, 61 percent of Americans, both Democrats and Republicans, agree with the public's negative perception of colleges and universities.[74]

Earlier in this chapter, Raymond Rickman, who was a college professor, was quoted as saying he thought colleges and universities were in the process of bringing about their own downfall, and that this would eventually happen because of a self-inflicted wound. The wound Rickman alluded to is the liberal bias that disconnects institutions of higher education from the society that picks up their tab and they are supposed to serve. Add to this the fact a college education has become almost impossibly expensive for the typical American family, and that institutions of higher education continue to turn out graduates with unmarketable degrees, and you have the perfect storm for the implosion of academia.

The quality of teaching and learning is diminished.

As the cost of college continues to increase, liberal bias may be reducing the quality of a college education. When only one point of view is allowed, the quality of teaching and learning is bound to suffer. In a *Chicago Tribune* article titled "The problem with all those liberal professors," Cass Sunstein wrote that when there is a dominant political philosophy, students are less likely to receive a quality education and faculty members are less likely to learn from one another. Instead, students and professors find themselves in something best described as an information cocoon. If the political science faculty of a university consists almost exclusively of Democrats, one doubts students will enjoy the benefit of exposure to a wide range of views and opinions.[75]

The "Guilty by Reason of Whiteness" Fraud

One of the worst frauds ever perpetrated by socialists in academia is the "guilty by reason of whiteness" propaganda that's all the rage now in America's colleges and universities. Socialists call the concept "white privilege." For example, a sociology professor at Dartmouth University is trying to make a course in black history/white privilege mandatory for all students. The course is supposed to help white students, no matter how unbiased they may be, realize how bigoted they really are. This professor hopes to convince white students they are blind to the privileges of their skin color.

According to this Dartmouth professor, even when success depends on working hard and working smart, the cards are systemically stacked against people of color. She seems oblivious to what this says about people of any race other than Caucasian. Is she claiming people of color are incapable of working hard and working smart? A long list of black Americans who have built successful lives for themselves and their families suggests otherwise. How does she explain the meritocratic system people of color have used to excel in sports in this country? You don't become a top performer in Major League Baseball, the National Football League, or the National Basketball Association by claiming racial privilege. Rather, you have to consistently outperform everyone else who wants your position, regardless of their race.

Is this Dartmouth professor claiming white people who grew up in poverty, came from broken homes, and had to overcome all the inherent obstacles that go with these circumstances, are privileged? One of the veterans interviewed for this book found this kind of thinking particularly offensive. He never knew his father, and his mother simply walked out of the hospital after he was born, leaving him to be handed over to the foster care system. He was bounced from one foster family to another for years. His clothing came from the charity boxes of local churches, he had to fight for what little food he got, and he was surrounded by drugs, drug addicts, and drug pushers throughout his formative years.

As soon as he turned eighteen, this veteran joined the Marine Corps to escape an abusive foster father who wanted to use him as a drug "mule" and an alcoholic foster mother intent on abusing him sexually. Having extracted himself from the "privileged" conditions of his childhood, this veteran built a new life for himself by applying the Christian work ethic. He quickly rose through the ranks in the Marine Corps, earned a college degree, and eventually became what the corps calls a mustanger (an enlisted person who meritoriously earns a commission as an officer).

By the time he retired from the Marine Corps, this veteran was a Lieutenant Colonel. Following his retirement, he became a teacher and coach. When the subject of white privilege comes up in his presence, this veteran is quick to acknowledge he was and still is privileged, but not because of his race. Rather he is privileged to have had the opportunity to serve in the Marine Corps, live in a country that affords people like him opportunities to build better lives for themselves, and worship a God who was with him every day of his life, giving him the strength to endure the conditions he grew up in. It would be interesting to hear what the Dartmouth professor who believes in "guilty by reason of whiteness" would have to say about the privileged life of this veteran.

ANTI-CHRISTIAN, ANTICONSERVATIVE BIAS IN THE MEDIA

In his book *Unfreedom of the Press*, Mark Levin provides a detailed account of the history of journalism in this country. He makes the point that in its initial years, America had a press that extolled the virtues of the principles set forth in the Declaration of Independence and Constitution. Then came the era when newspapers openly supported one political party or the other and even chose names that made it clear which party they supported.[76] Journalistic objectivity came into being in the twentieth century. Journalists were supposed to report the news and allow readers to interpret it. Opinions were limited to the editorial page. Now in the twenty-first century, the press has cast aside any semblance of objectivity and become blatantly partisan, although it claims this is not the case.[77]

A free press, unfettered by government control or interference, is supposed to be a safeguard against tyranny, a barrier between politicians with nefarious agendas and American citizens whose liberty could be undermined by those politicians. So, what happens when the media becomes little more than a tool for politicians? What happens when the media steps over a line and instead of objectively informing Americans of facts, begins using its substantial influence to manipulate the facts in favor of a given ideology? These questions are important because they point out exactly what has happened with the press in America. The mainstream press and media have become little more than propaganda machines for the progressive movement.

According to Levin, "the mainstream media no longer promotes free speech or freedom of the press in spite of their claims to the contrary. Instead they have become political activists determined to encourage uniformity of thought based on progressive orthodoxy."[78] In other words, not only have the mainstream press and media become advocates for the progressive movement, but they have become determined, aggressive, and persistent allies.

Don't be confused by history here. Today's mainstream media outlets are not returning to those days when newspapers openly worked for specific political parties and even chose names to indicate which party. Today's mainstream media outlets have become the propaganda arm of the progressive movement. As such, they are hostile to conservative thought, but unlike their party-specific forerunners, they deny being politically biased. They hypocritically tell the American public they are reporting the facts, but this is hardly the case. According to Levin, people and groups who do not parrot the progressive narrative are dismissed or diminished. Those who toe the line of progressive orthodoxy are put on a pedestal and afforded favorable treatment.[79]

Press and media coverage of the Obama administration was overwhelmingly positive, with the mainstream media choosing to ignore or put a positive spin on the president's worse moments. Compare media coverage of the Obama administration with that of the Trump administration. More than 90 percent of the media coverage of Trump's presidency has been negative. According to *Investor's Business Daily*, the major news networks had a love affair with Obama but not with Trump. The coverage of Trump has been overwhelmingly negative, while his greatest accomplishment—revitalizing the economy—has been ignored.

In addition to the negative coverage of Trump, there is blatant liberal bias in the stories the mainstream media choose to cover. Media coverage of Trump has been highly selective. Throughout 2019 and in the run-up to the 2020 presidential election, most of the coverage of President Trump has focused on just five topics: the Russia investigation, immigration, the Brett Kavanaugh nomination, North Korea, and U.S.–Russia relations. Topics such as the economy, tax cuts, and deregulation were ignored or barely reported. According to *Investor's Business Daily*, the media no longer even attempt to be fair, balanced, or evenhanded. Instead, they openly support and promote the politics of the far left.[80]

The COVID-19 pandemic has been the latest cudgel the biased media has used to bludgeon President Trump with their accusations of everything from his being late in responding to the virus outbreak to his having started it.

CHAPTER 9

Disrespect for the Flag and the National Anthem

The premise: "While I fully understand the legal rights of individuals to ignore our National Anthem and show disdain for the American flag, these actions show profound disrespect for the hundreds of thousands of veterans who served our country, many of whom were wounded or died to protect the very freedoms those who disrespect our flag and anthem take for granted. We can only pray that one day Americans will regain the spirit of national unity, love of country, and responsibility that goes with the blessing of freedom."

—TOM RICE, U.S. Army, 1969–1996

*T*he veteran who expresses the premise for this chapter is Sergeant Tom Rice. Sergeant Rice is a veteran of both Desert Shield and Desert Storm. He retired from the U.S. Army reserve in 1996 as a First Sergeant. Among his many military awards are the Southwest Asia Service Medal with two Bronze Service

Stars and the Saudi Arabian Kuwait Liberation Medal. In 2017, Sergeant Rice was inducted into the Florida Veterans' Hall of Fame. As a civilian, Rice is a restaurant owner who devotes his free time and energy to supporting veterans, active-duty service members, and their families. He is a board member of Florida Veterans, Inc., an organization dedicated to making Florida the most veteran-friendly state in the U.S.

Rice's service to active-duty military members, veterans, and their families is legendary. Among the many projects he helped bring into reality include the Fisher House of the Emerald Coast, the Veterans Tribute Tower in Fort Walton Beach, Bob Hope Village (for widows of Air Force veterans), and the We Honor Veterans program in conjunction with Covenant Care. Rice also helped organize the Emerald Coast Honor Flight program for World War II veterans and serves on the military academy appointments board for Senator Marco Rubio.

Lack of Respect for Our National Symbols

Our featured veteran for this chapter, Rice, makes an important distinction between what is legal and what is right when it comes to America's flag and the National Anthem. Just because the First Amendment allows people to show disdain for the flag, the National Anthem, and our country doesn't mean they should. This sentiment was shared by the veterans interviewed and surveyed for this book. Their message was clear: You cannot disrespect the flag or the National Anthem without disrespecting the soldiers, sailors, airmen, guardsmen, and Marines who fought and died to protect your freedom to dissent.

In July 2019, open-border advocates stormed a U.S. Immigration and Customs Enforcement (ICE) facility in Aurora, Colorado. They tore down the American flag and replaced it with the Mexican flag. Their protest was not well received by local citizens, the veterans interviewed for this book, or Americans in general. In fact, local citizens soon rescued and replaced the American flag that had been torn down. One of the veterans we interviewed suggested protestors who tear down the American flag and replace it with the Mexican flag should be deported to Mexico. This veteran said this sad incident in Colorado is reminiscent of the anti-Vietnam War protests on college campuses all across America in the 1960s.

We are old enough to remember those protests. Campus protestors went beyond just showing disrespect for the American flag; they often burned and otherwise desecrated the very symbol of our nation. Observing college students abusing their freedom of expression by desecrating the very symbol of that freedom was hard to take, particularly for us and our fellow warriors who were serving under that flag at the time.

One of the veterans interviewed for this book called the antiwar protests of the 1960s one of the low points in America's history. But according to this veteran, the current protests against the flag and the National Anthem are just as bad and perhaps even worse. His rationale is that although the student protests of the 1960s were, in his opinion, self-serving, at least they were aimed at a specific war rather than at our country. When the draft was eliminated, antiwar protests on college campuses evaporated almost overnight. This reaction suggests what the antiwar protestors were really demonstrating against was being drafted and being sent to Vietnam rather than the war itself. The protests of today, on the other hand, are aimed at the very core of what it means to be an American.

There were many ways the college students of the 1960s could have expressed their opposition to the Vietnam War without abusing the symbol of the country that gave them the right to protest. One of the veterans from our survey, commenting on the Vietnam War protests, said, as a college student, he once asked a protestor what he thought would happen to him if he traveled to Hanoi and burned the flag of that communist country. The only answer he got was an indifferent shrug that conveyed the message "Who cares?" Like those who disrespect our flag and anthem today, this protestor took for granted the freedoms he enjoyed as an American and cared little about the broader meaning of his actions.

Our country was briefly united under the flag by the terrorist attacks on America on September 11, 2001. Americans of all political persuasions felt a burst of national pride as members of the New York City Fire Department hoisted a huge American flag over the smoldering rubble of what had been the Twin Towers. Bumper stickers quickly sprung up declaring "9-11: We will never forget." These bumper stickers were proudly displayed by Americans of all stripes and political persuasions. Unfortunately, many who claimed they would never forget quickly forgot. After a brief patriotic interlude, we found ourselves in a new era of disrespect for America's national symbols and, truly, America itself.

Brief History of America's Flag and National Anthem

As children, we learned the history of America's flag and the National Anthem at the same time as we learned the ABCs. Unfortunately, this is no longer the case. As a result, many of the protestors who refuse to honor the flag and anthem have no idea what these symbols stand for, how they came into being, or why it is important to honor them. The United States spends more than $600 billion per year on public education, yet many youngsters today know nothing about the flag and National Anthem. One of the veterans interviewed for this book called this a national disgrace.

On June 14, 1777, the second Continental Congress passed a resolution establishing the official flag of the thirteen United States. That flag was to be composed of thirteen alternating red and white stripes and thirteen white stars on a blue background. The new flag was first flown in battle on August 3, 1777 during the siege of Fort Stanwix during America's War of Independence.

Because the flag resolution passed by the Continental Congress did not specify the arrangement of the stars, some early flags had them arrayed in rows and columns while another—known as the Betsy Ross flag—had the stars arranged in a circle. (This is the version of the flag that offended onetime NFL quarterback Colin Kaepernick so much that Nike halted production of sneakers bearing its image.) The lack of specificity led to the making of many different versions of the flag in the early days of our nation.

Over the years, the flag went through many transformations as stars were added when new states joined the Union. Regardless of the configuration of the flag at any given point in history, the stars and stripes on it are symbols. The thirteen stripes represent the original thirteen colonies/states, and the stars represent the states. The white stripes represent purity and innocence, the red stripes represent hardiness and valor, and the blue setting for the stars represents vigilance, perseverance, and justice. All of these symbolic representations have been personified by the men and women who have served our country in uniform, and they continue to be personified by those who are serving now.

The National Anthem, or "The Star-Spangled Banner," grew out of a poem written by Francis Scott Key during the bombardment of Fort McHenry on September 14, 1814. The War of 1812 was still raging, and it wasn't going well for America. The Battle of Baltimore was being pressed by the British Navy, which was bombarding Fort McHenry in Baltimore's harbor. But the mighty British Navy was unable to subdue the fort. When the dust and smoke of battle cleared, the American flag—tattered and torn—still waved over the battered but unbeaten fort.

The sight of that flag waving defiantly and majestically over Fort McHenry inspired Key to write "The Star-Spangled Banner." Key's poem, put to music, eventually became America's National Anthem by an act of Congress on March 3, 1931. From that moment forward, whenever the National Anthem is played or sung, the proper response has been to stand erect and place your right hand over your heart. Kneeling or assuming any posture other than standing is a gesture of disrespect for the flag, what it stands for, and those brave Americans who have defended it in battle.

NFL Kneeling Phenomenon

Colin Kaepernick of the San Francisco 49ers is the player most closely associated with the kneeling phenomenon in the NFL. But he wasn't the first NFL quarterback to use kneeling to make a statement. That quarterback was Tim Tebow of the New York Jets and Denver Broncos. Kaepernick kneeled to protest what he saw as the ills of a nation unworthy of the respect standing for the National Anthem symbolizes. Tebow, on the other hand, knelt to thank God for blessing him with the good fortune to be an American and to play in the NFL.

Tebow's humble, respectful gesture pleased Christians but raised the hackles of thin-skinned unbelievers who quickly label-ed reverently kneeling on the field to thank God as "Tebowing." The label wasn't meant as a compliment. Grumbling over Tebow's gesture of gratitude to God was almost comical to listen to, as ill-informed and obviously biased commentators struggled to find reasons to criticize a gesture many Americans and NFL viewers agreed with, supported, and admired.

A number of other players followed Tebow's example and began kneeling in gratitude to God after scoring or making a good play. Some simply pointed toward heaven. Regardless of how the players showed their gratitude to the God who had blessed them with athletic talent and an opportunity to play professional football, liberal commentators tried to find reasons to criticize. When Tebow's five-year career in the NFL ended, the controversy over "Tebowing" quickly faded into the back-ground. Then along came Colin Kaepernick.

Like Tebow, Kaepernick used kneeling to make a statement, and as in Tebow's case, Kaepernick's gesture raised eyebrows. In fact, it soon raised a firestorm NFL officials and a number of team owners did not anticipate. Then they made matters worse by mishandling the situation. Soon other players were joining Kaepernick on their knees as the National Anthem played. What eventually got the attention of NFL officials was the fact that as players showed their disrespect by kneeling, fans showed their disgust by walking; they refused to buy tickets to games and tuned out the NFL on television.

Disgusted by the disrespect shown by NFL players, fans switched their allegiance to college football and professional baseball or simply turned off the television. As a result, NFL viewership, already in trouble before Kaepernick began his kneeling protests, took a serious dip. Patriotic Americans who resented seeing players kneel during the National Anthem stayed away from their favorite stadiums or changed the channel. Their message to NFL officials was clear: "We tune in to watch football, not to watch overpaid players make misguided political statements."

Kaepernick and his fellow kneelers were so disconnected from their fans and everyday Americans, they misjudged how their actions would be interpreted. This time those doing the grumbling about kneeling on the field weren't a few misguided anti-Christian commentators, as in the case of Tebow. Rather, the disenchanted were hundreds of thousands of longtime NFL fans who thought kneeling during the National Anthem was disrespectful. This time those who were disenchanted had currency; they could simply tune out the NFL and let its ratings plummet, which they did.

First, kneeling during the National Anthem was viewed as being disrespectful to the America that has blessed NFL players with an opportunity to play professional football. Everyday Americans found it difficult to grasp how people who could earn millions playing what in essence is a game had anything to complain about when they, the fans, had to work hard every day to eke out a decent living. Come the weekend, these fans wanted to enjoy a pleasant distraction from their daily grind watching a game most of them would give anything to play.

What they didn't want to see was the spectacle of players they would gladly switch places with use the game to make political statements. As one of the veterans interviewed for this book commented, fans thought the players should keep their politics out of the game. This veteran spoke for many when he said NFL players should stand up, shut up, and play football. Another said if he was interested in viewing political statements, he would watch cable talk shows rather than football games.

Kneeling during the National Anthem was supposed to send the message that America is a nation unworthy of respect because of the supposed lingering effects of slavery as well as other supposed issues of inequality and unfairness. One of the veterans in our survey commented on how disingenuous it was for a second-string quarterback who earned $39 million in three years with the San Francisco 49ers to claim he was protesting the inequities of American society. This veteran claimed a real inequity is that the interest earned on $35 million for just one year amounts to more than he had earned during his entire career in the military.

Americans, including the veterans we interviewed and surveyed, almost universally supported the right of protestors to make their grievances known concerning what they perceived as America's shortcomings. One of the veterans interviewed for this book spoke for many Americans when he said the NFL kneelers had every right to protest but should have found a more appropriate venue. They should have chosen an approach that could not be interpreted as a lack of respect for military personnel who at that very time were fighting and dying in Afghanistan, or for veterans who went in harm's way in other conflicts. This veteran made the point that failing to predict the negative reaction of Americans to kneeling showed either incredible naivety on the part of the players or just plain hubris.

At the peak of the NFL kneeling phenomenon, 64 percent of Americans thought the gesture was disrespectful to active-duty military personnel, veterans, and their families. When disgruntled NFL players staged one of their kneeling protests on national Gold Star Mother's Day, whether out of inexcusable ignorance or blatant callousness, their supposed cause lost even more credibility in the eyes of the American public. Now the kneelers were viewed not just as unpatriotic but as uncaring.

Gold Star Mother's Day is set aside to honor the mothers of military personnel killed in battle. One of the veterans interviewed for this book wondered what Gold Star mothers must have thought when they heard about NFL players dishonoring the very flag their children died fighting for. The level of insensitivity or ignorance required to disrespect the flag on such an important and painful day is mind-boggling. The flag NFL kneelers dishonored on Gold Star Mother's Day is the same flag covering the coffins of the dead children of these grieving mothers. If the players knelt on this hallowed day out of ignorance, their act was shameful. If they knelt out of insensitivity, their act was unforgivable.

A poignant moment occurred during the height of the NFL kneeling phenomenon prior to a game in Pittsburgh. Rather than stand for the National Anthem, the team waited in the locker room until it was over. Only one lone player, Alejandro Villanueva, came out of the locker room to stand for the National Anthem. He courageously chose to do the right thing in spite of pressure from his fellow players and coach. It turns out Villanueva had served in the military as an Army Ranger. Some of his fellow soldiers had come home in caskets draped with the very flag his teammates were refusing to honor. Again, the protestors misjudged public perception. As a result of this incident, NFL attendance declined further, but sales of Villanueva's jersey went up, way up.

A Veteran Speaks Out

"I grew up in South Florida and even enlisted in the military in Coral Gables, so my favorite NFL team has always been the Miami Dolphins. But that changed when Dolphin players started kneeling during the National Anthem. That is the most disrespectful gesture imaginable. I haven't watched a Dolphins game since the first player knelt during the anthem."

—BUD CORBETT, *U.S. Air Force, 1961–1984*

Senior Master Sergeant (retired) Corbett served on active duty for twenty-three years. After retiring from the Air Force as a Senior Master Sergeant, he embarked on a second career as a deputy sheriff for twenty-five years.

The NFL kneeling phenomenon wasn't just disrespectful, which league officials did not seem to care about; it was also bad for business, which league officials did care about. Their weak response to the kneeling protests appeared even worse when John Tortorella, a coach in the National Hockey League (NHL), stated unequivocally that any of his players who dishonored the flag by sitting during the National Anthem would be sitting on the bench for the whole game.[81] Here was a coach willing to take an unequivocal stand for the flag and National Anthem while indecisive NFL officials could only fumble the ball.

In November 2019, Colin Kaepernick was given an opportunity to work out in front of any NFL teams interested in signing him to a contract. But negotiations about when and where the workout would take place immediately fell apart, with Kaepernick's side claiming the whole thing was a charade to make it look like the NFL was giving the former quarterback a chance when it really wasn't. The NFL, of course, denied this allegation. As a result, the Kaepernick workout achieved little more than engulfing him and the NFL in controversy once again.

Maybe Kaepernick still has a future in football, but that remains to be seen. However, in the midst of the workout controversy, one thing became clear. Kaepernick missed football and wanted to play again. If he signs with an NFL team, one can only pray the experience of being out of football might humble him to the point he finally realizes what a blessing he had and lost. This, in turn, might give him a more respectful attitude toward the National Anthem of the country that gave him an opportunity thousands of young men can only dream of having.

Perhaps the worst aspect of the NFL kneeling phenomenon is that, as it was dying down in professional football, it was spreading into Olympic sports, high school football, and youth sports. An American Olympic fencer chose to kneel during the National Anthem in spite of the fact he represented the United States on the world stage. High school football teams took up the kneeling fad even though few of the players could articulate why they were kneeling. Worse yet, several players who were interviewed didn't even know the words to the National Anthem or anything about its history. They were kneeling in imitation of their role models in the NFL.

When Colin Kaepernick's NFL career and the kneeling phenomenon appeared to be over, the fans began to return to the stadiums (until all games were shut down by the coronavirus). Ticket sales were going up and television viewership was on the rise, trends that should continue in the aftermath of the COVID-19 pandemic. By and large, NFL fans respect the American flag, the National Anthem, and military veterans, even when some of their favorite players don't. There is a lesson in this that NFL executives and team owners should take to heart.

Megan Rapinoe Joins the Fray

The NFL kneeling phenomenon eventually lost momentum when Colin Kaepernick was let go by the San Francisco 49ers and failed to be picked up by any other NFL team. But Kaepernick's departure from professional football hardly signaled the end of an era characterized by disrespecting the American flag and the National Anthem. In the wake of the NFL kneeling phenomenon, another individual made headlines as she used her athletic fame as a platform for proclaiming her grievances against America in general and America's president in particular. This individual is a world-class athlete and the cocaptain of America's world champion Women's National Soccer Team: Megan Rapinoe.

Rapinoe refuses to place her hand over her heart during the National Anthem. When asked why, she responded that she would probably never put her hand over her heart or sing the National Anthem. Rapinoe claims her protests are aimed primarily at President Trump, but according to Marc Thiessen of *The Washington Post*, her protests began in September 2016, before Trump was elected. In claiming her protests are aimed strictly at President Trump, she may be trying to deflect the kind of criticism the NFL kneelers received from veterans and NFL fans who saw their gesture as disrespectful. But even if her grievances are solely with President Trump, Rapinoe is missing an important point.

Thiessen wrote that Rapinoe has a constitutional right to express her opposition to President Trump, a contention with which the veterans in our survey and interviews universally agreed. But the point she is either missing or ignoring is she doesn't play for the Trump administration; she plays for Team USA. When NFL players kneel during the National Anthem, it's disturbing, but at least they play for San Francisco, Dallas, Pittsburgh, Miami, Tampa, Seattle, Los Angeles, or other teams tied to specific cities, not for Team USA. Consequently, their misguided actions are not as disturbing as a member of Team USA refusing to honor the very flag she wears on her jersey. Many of our veterans agreed with Thiessen that if Rapinoe cannot show proper respect for the flag she represents, she shouldn't play for Team USA.[82]

Nike's Patriotic Shoe Fiasco

In 2019, Nike decided to release a shoe honoring America on the Fourth of July. The shoe had a replica of America's Revolutionary War-era flag on the heel. Nike chose the version typically referred to as the Betsy Ross flag, as noted previously. When Nike came up with this promotional idea, little had been heard from Colin Kaepernick since the demise of his NFL career. But upon learning about Nike's patriotic shoe, he objected, complaining the flag chosen by Nike had flown at a time when slavery was deeply embedded in America's culture. He is not alone in using slavery as the basis of protests. In the view of many socialists, America's past struggles with slavery make the United States a nation forever shamed. To them, slavery is both a permanent stain on America's conscience and a weapon they can use to attack our country.

A Veteran Speaks Out

"Dishonoring the flag and anthem is part of the progressive agenda. A progressive movement would mean making continued progress and steady improvement for society. The improvement could be made by political action or other reforms. Progress would be measured based on a common understanding of traditional American values. The current so-called progressive movement has selected its own definition of 'American values' and integrated that definition into their use of 'progressive' to give it wider public acceptance. The U.S. Constitution is what they should use for defining American values. As a U.S.A.F. officer, I swore an oath to defend the Constitution against all enemies, foreign and domestic. I view the 'progressive' agenda as a domestic threat. The so-called progressives are undermining traditional American values such as individual freedom, personal responsibility, self-reliance, positive work ethic, competition, and the rule of law."

—*GORDY FORNELL, U.S. Air Force, 1958–1993*

Lieutenant General (retired) Fornell had a distinguished thirty-five-year career in the Air Force, during which he flew more than fifty kinds of aircraft, logged more than seven thousand hours of flight time, earned parachute wings, and was certified as a Level III program manager.

They refuse to acknowledge the United States eliminated slavery at the cost of hundreds of thousands of American lives. Among other things they conveniently overlook is, as of 2019, there are fifty-two black members of Congress, and since 1870 more than 150 blacks have served in Congress. Worst of all, they ignore the fact that in 2008, America elected a black president. These facts do not represent perfection, but they do represent progress. Unfortunately, so-called progressives refuse to acknowledge progress when it comes to this issue.

Apparently, when Kaepernick complained about the flag on Nike's new shoe, nobody thought to mention versions of that flag had been flown by Union troops during America's Civil War, troops who were fighting and dying to end slavery. Nike officials quickly caved in to political correctness and recalled the "flag shoe." The company hardly covered itself in new glory by removing Old Glory from their shoe. Rather than just admit they caved in to political correctness, Nike offered the feeble excuse that the shoe had been removed because the flag on it was an old version, as if no one at the company knew that when choosing it.

One might reasonably ask why, if this was really the reason for recalling the flag shoe, Nike officials didn't then reissue the shoe with the current version of the American flag on it or, better yet, the version of the American flag flown on the day Abraham Lincoln signed the Emancipation Proclamation. When an organization has to make such lame excuses to justify its actions, it needs to rethink its actions.

Why It Is Important to Show Respect for America's National Symbols

Even as children, the veterans who participated in the development of this book understood saluting the flag and standing during the National Anthem are ways of showing respect to the United States of America. As they grew older, they learned that living in America meant having opportunity, freedom, fair competition, the rule of law, personal responsibility, and religious liberty. This knowledge solidified their respect for our country. Several of the veterans commented that every school day of their childhood began with the Pledge of Allegiance to the flag, and there was no controversy about it. The pledge was one of the first things they learned in school.

But it's been so long since public schools have allowed the Pledge of Allegiance to be recited, a generation grew up without learning to respect the nation that has blessed them so richly and given them unrivaled opportunities to build better lives for themselves. This ignorance of the blessings of liberty contributes to the success socialists enjoy, because it allows them to mislead gullible people who are susceptible to lies, half-truths, misdirection, and obfuscation. How socialists can expect perfection from a nation made up of imperfect people, including them, is a mystery.

We can, though, provide a clue to help solve this mystery. One of the foundational beliefs of secular humanists is people can be perfected and utopia can be achieved on earth. Ignoring the fact that thousands of years of evidence refute this belief, there is another problem with the progressives' utopian dream: Socialists have appointed themselves as the final arbiters of how perfection is defined and what it looks like. The rest of us have no say in the matter. But one thing we are sure of is this:

Perfection to a progressive is not the state of the America envisioned by the founders.

This is why it is so important for Americans to learn at a young age to show respect for our country's national symbols. When you disrespect the symbols, you disrespect America. When you disrespect America, you disrespect the men and women who have fought and died protecting our country and your liberty. Here are several reasons it is important to show respect for our national symbols.

- *It shows your appreciation for the blessings of liberty the founders put their lives and "sacred honor" on the line to provide for you.* There are more than 190 sovereign nations in the world. None of their citizens enjoys the level of individual rights, freedom, and liberty every American enjoys. Unfortunately, too many Americans don't appreciate the freedom and liberty our nation provides. Instead, they take it for granted. As one of the veterans in our survey commented, when the National Anthem is played, it's a good idea to spend those few minutes reflecting on what a blessing it is to live in a nation founded on individual rights and freedom.

- *It shows respect for the Americans who have fought and died defending your freedom, rights, and liberty.* More than a million men and women in uniform have paid the ultimate price for the freedom, rights, and liberty we enjoy as American citizens. Unfortunately, there are now Americans who blatantly disrespect the flag and National Anthem those heroes died defending. Kneeling when the National Anthem is played shows more than just disrespect for our nation; it shows a lack of gratitude to those who paid the ultimate price defending our liberty.

- *It encourages Americans to focus on what we have in common rather than the issues dividing us.* America is one of the most diverse nations in the world. We are a nation of legal immigrants whose world-views span the spectrum when it comes to politics, religion, and other big-ticket issues. But what has traditionally united us is the melting pot theory. In no other nation in the world can you come from somewhere else and be fully, proudly, and unequivocally accepted as not just a full-fledged citizen but one of us, a member of the family. What has historically united us in our pluralistic society is adherence to a common set of aspirations and values. It has long been this common set of aspirations and values that has melted us together; hence the melting pot theory. We all aspire to build better lives for ourselves and our families. In striving to build better lives, we have traditionally subscribed to a common set of values, including individual freedom, religious liberty, equality of opportunity, personal responsibility, self-reliance, a positive work ethic, fair competition, and the rule of law. Showing disrespect for our national symbols is showing disrespect for the values that are supposed to unite us, should unite us, and can still unite us.

- *It shows respect for what America aspires to be as a nation, rather than focusing on the imperfections our country works hard to overcome.* People who disrespect our national symbols like to justify their actions by pointing out America's shortcomings and imperfections. This is ironic coming from people who are themselves imperfect. Every human being ever born is flawed in some way. There is no perfection this side of heaven. Consequently, a country of the people, by the people, and for the people is going to be an imperfect country. What is important is not what we were at any given point in our national history, but what we want to be and are striving to become. Rather than focus solely on America's flaws, we should be thankful for the flaws we have overcome. What is important is the vision of the founders and the progress we have made toward achieving it, not the ways in which we fall short because we are imperfect people.

- *It shows respect for America as a nation, not for whoever is currently serving as president or in Congress.* Presidents come and go after no more than eight years. No matter who is serving as president at a given time, some Americans love him, some hate him, and some can't decide. Further, some love him today and hate him tomorrow. This is the nature of life in our constitutional republic. Although they often remain in office much longer than presidents, the same can be said for members of Congress: Some love them, some hate them, and some can't decide. But we stand for the National Anthem and flag not to honor the individuals who are in office at any given point in time but to honor the offices, the government of the people

they represent, and our nation. We honor the
fact America is a free country, not a dictatorship.
Although we will always be disenchanted with
certain government officials, we honor the fact that
as Americans we at least have a voice in electing
them.

- *It sets a positive and unifying example for others.*
When people of diverse backgrounds, beliefs,
worldviews, and cultures all stand together to
honor America's National Anthem and flag, it
sets an example for people at home and abroad.
Even more important, it shows our enemies we
are united in spite of our differences. In a diverse
nation such as America, nothing good will come
from separating ourselves into warring cliques
based on race, religion, national origin, or culture.
Tribalism is the opposite of what America stands
for: *E pluribus unum* ("out of many, one"). Love of
country and belief in the values it stands for have
long united Americans in spite of their diversity.
Honoring our national symbols demonstrates love
of country in a way others who are unsure of where
they stand can observe and learn from. Young
people are not born loving our country; they
have to learn to love it. Seeing adults of different
backgrounds, races, genders, income levels, ages,
occupations, and education levels stand together
to honor our national symbols sets an edifying
example for young people, an example that helps
them learn to love America.

The Truth About "Unfairness" in America

Socialists who attack America as a nation unworthy of respect often base their attacks on America's supposed unfairness. One of the veterans interviewed for this book complained she was tired of hearing America described by socialists as a nation founded by old white men for old white men. This veteran, who loves America, served our country for thirty years in the military, and as a racial minority finds it especially offensive to hear the United States described in this way. She commented how socialists often talk about unfairness, but what is really unfair is their purposeful ignoring of the blessings America provides its citizens.

Picking up on this theme, we decided to conclude this chapter with a few examples that show a different side of the fairness argument, a side socialists ignore.

- Rookie soldiers, sailors, airmen, guardsmen, and Marines (E-1s) earn around $19,200 per year. NFL rookies, on the other hand, including those who kneel during the National Anthem, earn a minimum of $480,000 per year. Is it really fair for such highly paid athletes to dishonor young Americans in uniform who are paid so little but do so much to protect them and their rights? Colin Kaepernick, the individual most closely associated with the NFL kneeling phenomenon, was paid $39 million during his three years with the San Francisco 49ers. During those same years, approximately nine thousand U.S. military personnel served in Afghanistan, earning a paltry sum by comparison, putting their lives on the line for the country he and his fellow kneelers chose to snub.

- Veterans who were surveyed and interviewed during the development of this book served in World War II and the wars in Korea, Vietnam, Iraq, Afghanistan, and a number of other hot spots around the globe. In just these few conflicts, more than five hundred thousand of our warriors came home in coffins draped with the American flag. Is it really fair for socialists to dishonor these courageous warriors and their families by refusing to show respect for the flag they fought under and died for? Asked another way, is it fair to use your right to protest in ways that dishonor those who fought and died to defend that right? Are there no other more appropriate ways to air your grievances?

- As of 2019, Congress is more racially and ethnically diverse than it has ever been. Nonwhites now make up 22 percent of the membership of Congress, and women account for 23.7 percent. In addition, in 2008 America elected a black president who, prior to the presidential election, had been a U.S. Senator. This being the case, is it really fair for socialists to dishonor the flag and anthem based on the claim America is a nation run by white men for white men?

We live in a fallen world populated by imperfect people. Consequently, life is not fair; it never has been and never will be. However, since the establishment of our country, Americans have worked hard and persistently to make life as fair and equitable as possible for all citizens. The equality of all Americans is the most fundamental tenet of the Declaration of Independence: "We hold these truths to be self-evident, that all men are created equal, that they are endowed by their Creator with certain unalienable rights, that among these are Life, Liberty, and the pursuit of Happiness…"

The first eight of the original ten amendments to the Constitution were written to protect individual American citizens from unfairness on the part of the government. Since the addition of the Bill of Rights to the Constitution, the federal government has enacted numerous laws to guarantee housing, voting, employment, public access, competition, and opportunity are fair and equal for all Americans. For those who dishonor our national symbols because they claim life in America is unfair, we have one question: Where else in the world can you find a nation more committed to the ideal of fairness and equality for all of its citizens? The answer to this question is *nowhere*. This being the case, America and its national symbols deserve the respect of all Americans regardless of their political views.

Whatever Happened to Paying the Price for Freedom?

Freedom is not free. It never has been and never will be. The freedoms we have historically enjoyed in America—the same freedoms currently under attack by socialists—have been hard won. More than 1.3 million soldiers, sailors, airmen, guardsmen, and Marines have been killed fighting to establish and preserve the freedoms guaranteed to all Americans. Millions more have been wounded. Add to these the martyrs of the civil rights movement, and it becomes clear freedom comes at a price. But are Americans still willing to pay the price? Many are; a growing number are not. Those who want freedom but are unwilling to pay the price it demands play right into the hands of socialists, who are doing their best to undermine our freedom.

Perhaps the worst example of those who are unwilling to pay the price for freedom came from the NBA. During the development of this book, Hong Kong was engulfed in protests against the suppressive policies being inflicted on its citizens by communist China. When large-scale protests broke out, China's minions in Hong Kong quickly responded with violence. Police were seen on camera clubbing, teargassing, and even shooting protestors. But no matter how violent police bullying became, the people of Hong Kong persisted, refusing to give up the freedoms they had long enjoyed but that communist China was determined to take from them.

As the world watched in horror, communist China showed its true color. Not only is that color red, it is blood red, as China's response to the protests in Hong Kong demonstrated to an international television audience. In the midst of the turmoil, the general manager of one NBA team had the courage to speak out against China's violent response to the freedom-loving citizens of Hong Kong. Communist Chinese officials immediately responded to this individual's brief pro-Hong Kong message by threatening to cancel contracts with the NBA that could cost the league billions. The NBA hardly covered itself with glory when it became apparent from its tepid response the league valued its contracts with the communist giant more than the freedom of little Hong Kong.

This was when LeBron James stepped forward and raised his voice, a voice many in America viewed as a voice of courage, conviction, and freedom. James, perhaps the greatest player in the history of the NBA and certainly one of the most influential, already had a reputation for speaking out in favor of social justice on behalf of anyone whose freedoms he thought were being trampled. But this time James surprised the world and disappointed many of his most loyal fans by speaking out on behalf of communist China.

By standing with communist China against the freedom-seeking people of Hong Kong, James gave his imprimatur to a country guilty of arbitrary imprisonment, religious persecution (particularly against Christians), torture, censorship of the media, denial of free speech, the unexplained disappearance of people who speak out on behalf of freedom, and the mass detention of people deemed undesirable. Given a chance to stand tall for freedom and justice, James instead seemed to be throwing the freedom-seeking citizens of Hong Kong under the proverbial bus in favor of money.

One of the veterans interviewed for this book commented that perhaps someone should read Matthew 16:26 to James and the NBA's decision-makers. This verse asks two simple but profound questions: "For what will it profit a man if he gains the whole world and forfeits his soul? Or what shall a man give in return for his soul?" One can only wonder how LeBron James and the NBA management team would respond to Dr. Martin Luther King's statement "Injustice anywhere is a threat to justice everywhere."[83]

This willingness to sacrifice freedom for the sake of money is likely to continue and even become a growing problem as more and more U.S. companies open operations in China. Eventually, the maxim "Freedom has a price" may have to be replaced with "Your freedom is fine as long it doesn't cost me anything." This raises an important concern. How can our country expect young people in the prime years of their lives to go in harm's way to protect the freedoms guaranteed all Americans when prominent opinion makers like LeBron James and the NBA put their wallets ahead of freedom? This shameful episode in the history of the NBA bodes badly for the America envisioned by our founders.

CONCLUSION

Stand Up and Speak Out

The premise: *"Today's generation of millennials expect a lot, but with little effort on their part. They want things to come easily without having to work for and achieve results. This is disheartening, but I do not blame them solely for this attitude. I also blame those who are preparing our youth for the future. Coddling, overproviding, and accepting failure have replaced encouragement of working hard for what you want. For example, affluent teens have their parents buy their way into college instead of requiring them to earn admission based on grades and merit. Too many parents are enablers instead of requiring their children to experience the realities of life as naturally as possible. My military experience coupled with a solid foundation at home early on encouraged me to follow my own path and earn my way. I had no financial backing, just a determination to go forth and serve my country proudly, with the support of my family."*

—SHAWNI JONES, *U.S. Air Force, 1990–2014*

*O*ur *featured veteran for this concluding chapter is* Shawni Jones. Jones began her career in the Air Force in 1990 as a pharmacy technician at Sheppard Air Force Base, Texas, and continued in that field through 2006. In 2006 she cross-trained and became an emergency actions (EA) controller at Scott Air Force Base, Illinois. Her service as an EA controller took her to duty in Grand Forks, North Dakota, and Hickam Air Force Base, Hawaii. She completed her career in the Air Force as command and control manager for policies and procedures at Joint Base Pearl Harbor-Hickam, Hawaii.

One More Battle to Fight

Jones makes an important point when she states that the coddling of youngsters and accepting less than their best has given millennials an attitude toward life in which mediocrity is acceptable and expecting others to take care of them is normal. This attitude fits right in with where socialists are trying to take this country, because it makes millennials easy to manipulate. When they are told that in the America socialists envision the government will take care of them, millennials are all for it.

One of the veterans interviewed for this book made the point that although he fought many battles during his time in the military, he still had one more battle to fight, and that final battle might turn out to be the most important of them all. The battle he spoke of is not taking place on foreign soil or in distant waters. Rather, this battle is happening right here and right now in the United States of America. We are talking about the battle between those who love America and those who hate America. It is a battle for the soul of our nation, a battle not of guns, bombs, and missiles but of ideas, beliefs, and values.

The battle lines are clearly drawn. On one side you have Americans who love our country, believe it to be exceptional among the nations of the world, and think America is both great and good in spite of its imperfections. These are Americans who still believe in the nation envisioned by our founders, a nation with a strong moral foundation and positive core values. These values include individual freedom, religious liberty, equal opportunity, personal responsibility, self-reliance, a positive work ethic, fair competition, and the rule of law.

A Veteran Speaks Out

"While kneeling for the National Anthem is a protected right under the Constitution, as the son of a legal immigrant and as an Army combat veteran, I believe there is a better time and way to express that right. I served in the military to protect the right of individuals to dissent. However, I find it abhorrent that athletes would make our nation's symbols—the flag and National Anthem—the focal points of their protests."

—*ROBERT AMBROSE IKYASANG, U.S. Army, 1995–2000*

Ikyasang served as a multichannel transmission systems operator/maintainer, Bravo Company, 82nd Signal Battalion, 82nd Airborne Division.

Those who attack America from within refer to themselves as progressives, an ironic label since there is nothing progressive about their agenda for America. So-called progressives/socialists reject our country's Christian heritage and core values. To them, America is neither great nor good. Rather, they view our country as repressive, shameful, and unworthy of respect. Perhaps no other act so personifies the attitudes of socialists toward our country than showing disrespect to the flag and National Anthem. Of all the issues covered in our interviews and surveys, this is the one that raised the hackles of veterans most.

We now know that those who call themselves progressives are socialists who were previously trying to cloak their true identity and purpose: intentionally undermining traditional American values. They do this by advocating for socialist policies, attacking the Second Amendment, revising America's history to support their false narrative, rejecting morality based on Christian principles, favoring secular humanism and moral relativism, practicing the despicable tactics of personal destruction, resorting to character assassination in politics, lobbying for open borders, establishing sanctuary cities to protect illegal immigrants instead of American citizens, contributing to the ongoing coarsening of the culture, using higher education and the media to undermine Christian and conservative beliefs, and going out of their way to show disrespect for America's flag and National Anthem.

The battle between those who believe in the vision of America's founders and those who reject that vision is a battle we must win if our children, grandchildren, and great-grandchildren are going to inherit the blessings of freedom and liberty enjoyed by past generations. The utopia envisioned by socialists is a pipe dream that has failed everywhere it has been tried. Socialism is a concept doomed from the outset because it fails to take into account the flaws of human nature.

Young Americans join the military and agree to go in harm's way because they love our country. They love America because of what it means to them: freedom, liberty, opportunity, equality, fair competition, and the rule of law. Those who serve in uniform believe these things are worth fighting for and, if necessary, dying for. But what is going to happen if those who reject the America of the founders prevail in the current battle? Will America still be a country worth fighting and dying for? Will a generation raised to kneel during the National Anthem and disrespect the flag be willing to put themselves in harm's way to protect the nation these symbols represent?

We hope and pray that having read this book, you will join the millions of Americans who still believe in the vision of our founders and still subscribe to the traditional values that made America great. But reading this book is not enough. If you love America and want to preserve what is best about our country for future generations, join the millions of Americans who are determined to preserve and protect the founders' vision. Don't just sit on the sidelines wringing your hands in frustration. Don't give up in despair. Rather, do what the veterans who participated in the development of this book do: stand up and speak out.

Arm yourself with the information needed to refute the destructive schemes of the left and their false narrative of a repressive, unworthy America. We have provided that information in this book. Your challenge is to use this information on behalf of our country. Every time a young person who has never lived in a socialist country claims to prefer socialism to capitalism, stand up and speak out. Every time a misguided gun-control advocate blames guns for violence instead of the people who misuse them, stand up and speak out. When socialists try to revise history to fit their false narrative, stand up and speak out.

Instead of bending to pressure from the left to be politically correct, make a point of being patriotically correct. When socialists engage in the politics of destruction and character assignation, demand the truth. When progressive politicians advocate for open borders, remind them of whom they were elected to serve. When socialists bemoan the consequences of cultural coarsening, remind them they are simply reaping what they have sown, as are the rest of us. When institutions of higher education persecute Christians and conservatives, withhold your support from them. But don't stop there. Also demand that politicians withhold their state and federal dollars. Do not help finance the nefarious schemes of those who are trying to undermine the vision of the founders.

When media outlets spread socialist propaganda and call it news, change the channel or turn the television off altogether. Let the stations' declining ratings send them a message on your behalf. Finally, set a positive example of honoring America's flag and National Anthem, and call out those who don't. When professional athletes refuse to show respect for the flag or National Anthem, show your displeasure by changing the channel, staying home instead of going to the stadium, and no longer buying tickets.

When the stands are empty and management is no longer able to pay their ridiculously high salaries, these spoiled, misguided athletes might finally get the message. Let's see how strongly they feel about disrespecting our country and the veterans who fought for it when salaries are reduced and players are laid off because of poor ratings. It is easy to protest and dissent when it costs you nothing. Let's see how strongly kneeling athletes feel about their cause when more and more fans demonstrate their displeasure by tuning them out.

One of the veterans interviewed for this book claimed that we should change the title and wording of the song "God Bless America" to "God Help America." We understand this veteran's sentiments. Although it is our prayer God will indeed help America, we also pray He continues to bless America. Just as He has given protestors the right of dissent, God has given you the right to stand up and speak out on behalf of what is good about America. We encourage you to use this God-given and constitutionally reaffirmed right to pull America back from the abyss and restore it to the nation our founders envisioned.

To this end, we conclude with a passage from Scripture that reinforces our challenge to stand up and speak out to all Americans who believe in the vision of our Founding Fathers. This passage is Ephesians 6:13–18:

> Therefore take up the whole armor of God, that you may be able to withstand in the evil day, and having done all, to stand firm. Stand therefore, having fastened on the belt of truth, and having put on the breastplate of righteousness, and, as shoes for your feet, having put on the readiness given by the gospel of peace. In all circumstances take up the shield of faith, with which you can extinguish all the flaming darts of the evil one; and take the helmet of salvation, and the sword of the spirit, which is the word of God, praying at all times in the spirit, with all prayer and supplication. To that end, keep alert with all perseverance, making supplication for all the saints…

ENDNOTES

Chapter 1

1   George W. Bush, georgewbushwhitehouse.archives.gov on September 20, 2019.

2   Andrew Roberts, *Churchill: Walking with Destiny* (Viking, an imprint of Penguin Random House LLC: 2018), 887.

3   Nima Sanandaji, *Debunking Utopia: Exposing the Myth of Nordic Socialism* (WND Books: 2016).

4   America First Policies, "Securing Our Border," accessed July 10, 2019, https://www.americafirstpolicies.org/issues/securing-our-border/.

Chapter 2

5   John R. Lott, Jr., "A Look at the Facts on Gun-Free Zones," *National Review*, accessed July 2, 2019, www.nationalreview.com/2015/10/gun-free-zones-don't-save-lives-right-to-carry-laws-do.

6   FBI Uniform Crime Reporting, retrieved September 26, 2019, ucr.fbi.gov.

7   Benjamin Franklin (quoting Psalm 127:1), Speech to the Constitutional Convention, https://www.azquotes.com/quote/350015.

8   Thomas Jefferson, Notes on the State of Virginia, query 18 (1781–1785), https://www.azquotes.com/quote/519534.

9   John Jay, http://www.foundingfatherquotes.com/quote/675.

Chapter 3

10   Public Acts of the 32nd Congress, retrieved June 15, 2019, https://www.loc.gov/law/help/statutes-at-large/32nd-congress/c32.pdf.

11   "The Mayflower Compact," Pilgrim Hall Museum, accessed January 19, 2019, https://www.pilgrimhall.org/ap_mayflower_compact.htm.

12 Archie P. Jones, *America's First Covenant: Christian Principles in the Articles of Confederation* (Plymouth Rock Foundation, 1991), 7.

13 "Constitution of South Carolina, March 19, 1778," Yale Law School, accessed January 19, 2019, http://avalon.law.yale.edu/18th_century/sc02.asp.

14 Gary DeMar, *God and Government: Biblical, Historical, and Constitutional Perspective* (The American Vision, 2011), 183.

15 Ibid., 182.

16 A Constitution or Frame of Government Agreed Upon by the Delegates of the People of the State of Massachusetts-Bay (Boston: Benjamin Edes & Sons, 1780), 44, Chapter VI, Article I.

17 National Archives, "Declaration of Independence: A Transcription," accessed January 24, 2019, https://www.archives.gov/founding-docs/declaration-transcript.

18 Archie P. Jones, *Christian Principles in the Constitution and Bill of Rights: Part 1* (Plymouth Rock Foundation, 1991), 13.

19 John Dickinson, *The Political Writings of John Dickinson*, vol. I (Wilmington: Bonsal and Niles, 1801), 111–12.

20 John Adams, *The Works of John Adams, Second President of the United States*, vol. IX, ed. Charles Francis Adams (Boston: Little Brown & Company, 1854), 291. Adams' original correspondence was written in 1809.

21 Thomas Jefferson, Notes on the State of Virginia, Query XVIII, 237.

22 Monroe's second annual message to Congress, November 16, 1818. https://millercenter.org/the-presidency/presidential-speeches/november-16-1818-second-annual-message

23 Lewis Henry Boutell, *The Life of Roger Sherman* (Chicago: A. C. McClurg and Co., 1896), 272–73.

24 Archie P. Jones, *Christianity and Our State Constitutions, Declarations and Bills of Rights: Part I* (Plymouth Rock Foundation, 1991), 14.

Chapter 4

25 "Moral Relativism—Neutral Thinking?" accessed July 21, 2019, http://www.moral-relativism.com.

26 Ibid.

27 As quoted in: Ben Stein and Phil DeMuth, *Can America Survive?* (Carlsbad, California: New Beginnings Press, an imprint of Hay House, 2004), 111.

28 "Moral Relativism—Neutral Thinking?" accessed July 21, 2019, http://www.moral-relativism.com.

29 American Humanist Association, "Humanist Manifesto II," accessed July 7, 2019, https://americanhumanist.org/what-is-humanism/manifesto2.

30 Ibid.

31 *Humanism and Its Aspirations* (Washington, D.C.: American Humanist Association, 2003).

32 Ryan Dobson, *Be Intolerant: Because Some Things Are Just Stupid* (Carol Stream, Illinois: Tyndale House Publishers, 2003), 55.

33 Ibid., 55–56.

34 Ibid., 49.

35 Ibid., 50–55.

36 "Joseph Goebbels on the 'Big Lie,'" Jewish Virtual Library, https://www.jewishvirtuallibrary.org/joseph-goebbels-on-the-quot-big-lie-quote.

Chapter 5

37 Pew Research Center, "Partisanship and Political Animosity in 2016," accessed July 9, 2019, https://www.people-press.org/2016/06/22/partisanship-and-political-animosity-in-2016/.

38 Ibid.

39 Frank Newport and Andrew Dugan, "Partisan Differences Growing on a Number of Issues," accessed July 9, 2019, https://news,gallup.com/opinion/polling-matters/215210/partisan-differences-growing-number-issues.aspx.

40 Tom Brokaw, "Change was in the Air," foreword to *The 1960s—the Decade When Everything Changed* (*LIFE*, 2019), 6.

41 Pew Research Center, retrieved May 7, 2020, https://pewforum.org/2019/10/17/in-u-s-decline-of-christianity-continues-at-rapid-pace/.

42 R. Albert Mohler, Jr., "Harvard University's Founding Vision and Mission—A Timely Reminder," accessed

July 9, 2019, https://albertmohler.com/2006/02/22/harvard-universitys-founding-vision-and-mission-a-timely-reminder.

43 Walter Williams, "Being a racist is easy today," Opinion, *Northwest Florida Daily News*, July 31, 2019.

44 Ibid.

45 Ibid.

Chapter 6

46. America First Policies, "Securing Our Border," accessed July 10, 2019, https://www.americafirstpolicies.org/issues/securing-our-borders/.

47 David A. Clarke, Jr., "The Need for Secure Borders," *Townhall*, accessed July 9, 2019, https://townhall.com/columnists/sheriffdavidclarke/2018/04/11/the-need-for-secure-borders-n2469623.

48 America First Policies, "Securing Our Border," accessed July 10, 2019, https://www.americafirstpolicies.org/issues/securing-our-borders/.

49 David A. Clarke, Jr., "The Need for Secure Borders," *Townhall*, accessed July 10, 2019, https://townhall.com/columnists/sheriffdavidclarke/2018/04/11/the-need-for-secure-borders-n24696239.

Chapter 8

50 Elite Driving School, "Road Rage Statistics Filled With Surprising Facts," retrieved May 7, 2020, drivingschool.net/road-rage-statistics-filled-surprising-facts.

51 National Safety Council, retrieved May 7, 2020, nsc.org/work-safety/safety-topics/workplace-violence.

52 National Highway Traffic Safety Administration, retrieved July 17, 2019, nhtsa.gov/risky-driving/distracted-driving.

53 Centers for Disease Control, retrieved April 9, 2020, cdc.gov/drugoverdose/data/statedeaths.html.

54 Centers for Disease Control and Prevention, "America's Drug Overdose Epidemic: Data to Action," retrieved May 7, 2020, cdc.gov/injury/features/prescription-drug-overdose/index.html.

55 ABC News, "How to Handle 'Sideline Sports Rage,'" retrieved May 7, 2020, abcnews.go.com/GMA/ESPNSports/story?id=1034449&page=1.

56 Phyllis Schlafly, "Diversity Dishonesty on College Campuses," *The Phyllis Schlafly Report* 35, no. 9 (April 2002).

57 David Horowitz, "Academic Bill of Rights," accessed July 11, 2019, www.taup.org/taupweb2006/hr177/aborhorowitz.pdf.

58 Jerry Bergman, *Slaughter of the Dissidents* (Leafcutter Press, 2011).

59 As quoted in *Brainwashed: How Universities Indoctrinate America's Youth* (Nashville, Tennessee: WND Books, 2004), 85.

60 Ibid.

61 John Indo, "Logic for Fundamentalists?" *Free Inquiry* 2, no. 1 (Winter, 1981): 3.

62 Alliance Defending Freedom, "View our Cases," retrieved May 7, 2020, adflegal.org/for-attorneys/cases.

63 Alliance Defending Freedom, accessed on January 11, 2019,https://www.adflegal.org/press-release/judge-acquits-christian-charged-criminal-trespass-preaching-public-property .

64 Ibid.

65 Ibid.

66 Ibid.

67 Ibid.

68 Ibid.

69 Ibid.

70 James Barrett, "How Politically Biased Are Colleges? New Study Finds It's Far Worse Than Anybody Thought," *The Daily Wire*, accessed July 12, 2019, https://www.dailywire.com/news/30222/how-politically-biased-are-universities-new-study-james-barrett.

71 Allen C. Guelzo, "Free Speech and Its Present Crisis," *City Journal*, accessed July 11, 2019, https://www.city-journal.org/free-speech-crisis.

72 Ibid.

73 Jennifer Harper, "86% of university presidents cite negative effects of 'liberal political bias on campus': poll," *Washington Times*, accessed July 13, 2019, https://washingtontimes.com/news/2018/mar/14/86-of-university-presidents-cite-negative-effects-/.

74 Lauren Cooley, "Liberalism is rampant on campus and ruining academia," *Washington Examiner*, accessed July 13, 2019, https://www.washingtonexaminer.com/red-alert-politics/liberalism-is-rampant-on-campus-and-ruining-academia.

75 Cass R. Sunstein, "The Problem With All Those Liberal Professors," accessed July 13, 2019, https://www.bloomberg.com/opinion/articles/2018-09-17/colleges-have-way-too-many-liberal-professors.

76 Mark R. Levin, *Unfreedom of the Press* (Threshold Editions, an imprint of Simon & Schuster, 2019), inside front cover.

77 Ibid., 2.

78 Ibid.

79 Ibid.

80 "Media Trump Hatred Shows In 92% Negative Coverage of His Presidency: Study," Editorial, *Investor's Business Daily*, accessed July 15, 2019, https://www.investors.com/politics/editorials/media-trump-hatred-coverage/.

Chapter 9

81 Marc Thiessen, "Disrespecting the flag is a disgraceful way to protest Trump," *The Washington Post*, September 25, 2017.

82 Marc Thiessen, "Megan Rapinoe's anthem protests hurt the fight for gender equity," *The Washington Post*, July 5, 2019.

83 Cited on: https://thepeopleoftheworld.wordpress.com/injustice-anywhere-is-a-threat-to-justice-everywhere/.